STUDIES IN THE BRITISH ECONOMY

BRITAIN'S OVERSEAS TRADE

STUDIES IN THE BRITISH ECONOMY

by Derek Lee, Vivian S. Anthony and Allen Skuse

1. Monopoly
2. Regional Planning and Location of Industry
3. Britain's Overseas Trade

STUDIES IN THE BRITISH ECONOMY

Britain's Overseas Trade

The recent history of British trade, 1868-1968

by

Vivian S. Anthony

Economics master, Tonbridge School

HEINEMANN EDUCATIONAL
BOOKS LTD · LONDON

Heinemann Educational Books Ltd
LONDON EDINBURGH MELBOURNE TORONTO
AUCKLAND SINGAPORE JOHANNESBURG
HONG KONG NAIROBI IBADAN

SBN 435 84538 1

First published 1969

Published by Heinemann Educational Books Ltd
48 Charles Street, London W1X 8 AH
Printed in Great Britain by Cox and Wyman Ltd
London, Fakenham and Reading

PREFACE

Most economics text books attempt to cover the subject within a single volume and in consequence some topics are treated briefly: often these same topics are those whose subject matter changes most rapidly. At present in order to keep up to date in the field of economics recourse must be made to a vast field of diffused literature including bank reviews, government publications, newspapers and various journals. With these problems in mind this series was conceived. The series consist of specialised books on those topics which are subject to frequent change or where the sources of information are too scattered to be readily available to the average student. It is intended that each book will be revised at frequent intervals in order to take account of new developments.

The books are written with the needs of Advanced Level candidates especially in mind, but they also cover the ground for many professional examinations in economics.

Derek Lee
Vivian Anthony
Allen Skuse

AUTHOR'S NOTE

In common with the other books in Studies in the British Economy, *Overseas Trade* deals with recent developments in the subject. But the book also examines changes in the pattern of Britain's trade over the last hundred years. It attempts to make clear to students of Economics and Economic History the reasons for these changes, and the results of recent research in the subject, which is not always comprehensible to those who have recently begun to study the topic.

My thanks are due to the members of my VIth form who have helped me by reading the manuscript, suggesting charts and diagrams, and preparing the index.

Vivian Anthony

CONTENTS

CHAPTER 1

THE EMERGENCE OF THE MODERN PATTERN OF TRADE

Trade before 1868

In the course of the nineteenth century the pattern of Britain's overseas trade changed fundamentally, while the importance of trade in Britain's economic life continued to increase. In the centuries preceding the Industrial Revolution the dominant elements of Britain's export trade had changed from the export of basic materials – raw wool, skins, hides, minerals – to the export of staple secondary products, especially woollens. Although the import of manufactured goods continued to be important in this period, the growing need for foodstuffs and basic materials in Britain, and the expanding contribution of her colonies, was reflected in the import trade. The demands of industries during the Industrial Revolution produced a significant decline in the proportion of the nation's resources available to agriculture. At the same time the population explosion was making ever-increasing demands on the farmers. With limited resources available the comparative cost advantage of Britain's rapidly expanding industries, e.g. textiles, which accounted for 60 per cent of the total in 1850, metals, and coal, dictated that as the proportion of factors in specialist manufacturing trades increased, the products of these trades would have to be sold abroad in larger and larger quantities to pay for essential imports of food and basic materials. Britain's comparative advantage in the export of manufactured goods continued to increase and by the middle of the nineteenth century the rise in the value of Britain's exports allowed a considerable growth in the value of imports per head. These extra imports contributed to the improving standard of living in the period of Victorian prosperity.

Invisibles

The growth of Britain's overseas earnings by the middle decades of the nineteenth century was not solely attributable to the growth in the export of manufactured goods. Earnings from invisible items were increasing apace. As the volume and value of world trade increased, the earnings of Britain's shipping rose at least in proportion. British ships carrying abroad the products of Britain's expanding industries returned laden with commodities demanded by a growing population enjoying a rising standard of living. The naval traditions of these islands allowed the British mercantile marine to develop its cost advantages over the merchant navies of other countries and as a result British ships were increasingly used for carrying foreigners' exports to other foreigners. The net earnings of shipping, i.e. the difference between Britain's payments to others for carrying British goods and the payments of others to Britain for the services of her ships, were almost £20m in 1850, and by the end of the third quarter of the century they were over £50m. The capital invested in foreign countries by British citizens was another important source of income from abroad. In 1850 the interest on foreign investment was just over £10m, while in 1875 it was £50m. British traders and others earned further income on services performed abroad and these, along with the earnings of British insurance abroad, was the source of another £50m in 1875.

Balance of trade

The considerable size of Britain's invisible earnings enabled her to run a deficit on the balance of trade during most of the second half of the century. In the middle of the century Britain's imports exceeded her exports of home produced goods by more than £25m, while at the beginning of the last quarter the deficit was over £60m. The value of Britain's imports almost trebled in the third quarter of the century, with the proportion of foodstuffs increasing until it equalled the value of imported basic materials. The increased value of imports and exports owed little to changes in prices, so that it can be explained largely by the quantity of commodities bought and sold by this country. Prof. Imlah in *J.E.H.* 1950 has shown that there was little change in the level of export prices as a percentage of the level of import prices, that is in the NET BARTER TERMS OF TRADE.

Reasons for the growth of trade

The increase in the quantity of commodities bought and sold has been attributed to a variety of causes. The improvements in Britain's railways, and the export of her railway engineering products and expertise, brought about an improvement in transport facilities abroad, and further opened up these markets. This made possible greater exploitation of British connections. The railway materials were important British visible exports while the capital which financed this railway development overseas was often raised in Britain, and the interest provided valuable invisible earnings. The steam power used first to power the railway engines, was later applied to increase the efficiency of ships. The commodities in Britain's trade could then be carried in increased quantities, at greater speed and at lower costs, and the steam-driven ships could be sold to foreigners. Britain's period of comparative advantage in the building of steam ships was established before the end of the third quarter.

If improved transport facilities were an important factor in the opening up of foreign markets which enabled overseas trade to grow, the increased purchasing power of her foreign customers was also vital. Britain's free trade policy enabled them to find a market for their foodstuffs and raw materials in Britain unhindered by a tariff barrier. They benefited because the prices of their goods in Britain were lower than they would have been if import duties had been imposed. The British consumer showed his appreciation of the relatively low price of imported food by buying larger and larger quantities. Foreigners enjoying a rising income from commodities exported to Britain were able to spend more on the manufactured goods that Britain was exporting. The increased incomes of Britain's customers also stemmed from the economic activity stimulated by Britain's investment abroad, including the activity associated with the transport improvements mentioned above. As other countries reached the stage of the 'take-off' into industrialism Britain was in the position to exploit her comparative advantage in the provision of capital equipment. She was able to supply machines and expert technical knowledge in the basic industries of iron and steel, textiles and coal, just as she was doing in transport.

British enterprise

There was no lack of quality in the factor of production enterprise at this stage in Britain's economic history. Britain's entrepreneurs saw to it that the market opportunities that had been opened up were not wasted. They were usually not tardy in exploiting the improvements in productive techniques which were made possible by the inventors and innovators. In this way the costs of production per unit of output in Britain's basic industries were lowered and the comparative cost advantages of those industries increased. Nowhere was this advantage more spectacularly increased than in the production of steel.

The advantages arising from the favourable movements of comparative costs are often CUMULATIVE as factors of production are attracted to those industries which were making the most of the favourable market opportunities. The entrepreneur in the expanding industries was able to draw on supplies of capital more easily than ever before. We have already seen that the growing supplies of capital, and in particular, that part invested abroad, was the source of one of the main invisible earnings, namely the interest paid to British investors by foreign borrowers. The availability of capital for short term lending made possible the extension of the services performed in the finance of foreign trade and commerce, and the development of British financial institutions which specialized in these services, bringing further invisible earnings. Some of these invisible earnings were needed to pay for the growing deficit on the balance of trade, but not all these earnings were used to pay for increased imports; the remainder was reinvested abroad helping to accelerate the growth of consumer and producer demand in those countries for British goods.

SUMMARY

In summarizing the main trends which were evident in Britain's trade a century ago the following themes emerge:

1. In the preceding period the pattern of trade had undergone a fundamental change. Basic materials had become an unimportant part of the export trade, which was now dominated by manufacturers. Foodstuffs were rapidly catching up basic materials and luxury manufactured products as the country's main imports.

2. Manufactured goods accounted for almost 90 per cent of Britain's exports, and textiles was the dominant category contributing over 70 per cent of the total value of all exports. Iron goods, the next most important, formed just over 10 per cent of the total.

3. In the rapidly growing import trade, foodstuffs was the fastest rising category, and within this, dairy produce and wheat were showing the largest increases.

4. Although the value of Britain's visible imports and exports was expanding rapidly, having almost trebled in the 30 years previous to

1857, the growth of Britain's invisible earnings had not lagged behind, and was now almost up to two-thirds of the value of visible exports. Shipping, foreign investment and insurance, and trade services were equally important contributors to the total earnings.

5. British entrepreneurs had begun to exploit their comparative cost advantages in the manufacture and export of capital goods to the countries experiencing the 'take-off' into industrialism. To pay for these machines essential for their new industries, and the equipment necessary for the construction of a transport system, her foreign customers often borrowed in Britain.

6. The growing volume of Britain's exports was maintained by:

(*a*) The market opportunities consequent on increased purchasing power abroad.
(*b*) The reduction in costs per unit in the manufacture of our basic exports particularly textiles, and iron and steel, consequent on new inventions.
(*c*) The reduction in costs resulting from improvements in communications.
(*d*) The increasing supplies of capital in Britain, which were used to finance the trade.

7. The growing surplus of invisible earnings was being used to finance an increasing deficit on the balance of trade as the British pushed up their standard of living by importing the things they required. What remained after these extra imports had been paid for, was reinvested abroad, and the interest on this investment helped to swell future invisible earnings. Britain was making good use of a fundamentally favourable balance on the *current account of the balance of payments*, i.e. the surplus of export earnings visible and invisible over payments for imports visible and invisible, but not including the movement of long-term capital.

CHAPTER 2

BRITAIN'S TRADE – 1868-1914: PROSPERITY AND POWER

The volume of Britain's trade more than doubled in the period 1867–1916, exports and re-exports increasing by just over 100 per cent, while imports increased by some 120 per cent in volume. It would appear then, that the trends of the mid-Victorian era of prosperity (1850–75) continued until the beginning of the First World War. Exports continued to grow about as fast as the output of British manufactures, and helped Britain enjoy the benefits of a world economy increasing in prosperity.

A Great Depression

But the last quarter of the nineteenth century has been described by some economic historians as the 'Great Depression' and it is illuminating to reconcile the conflicting viewpoints. The comparative cost advantages enjoyed by British producers of basic manufactures such as textiles and metals were steadily eroded as foreign rivals learnt to produce these commodities cheaply. This was reflected in a very large fall in prices so that although the volume of Britain's exports continued to increase steadily the VALUE averaged over the last 5 years of the century (£14m) was only 5 per cent higher than average of the 5 years preceding the last quarter (£98m). A good deal more work was producing very little increase in returns from trade.

The importance of overseas trade in the British economy has often been exaggerated (see Chapter 3), but there is no doubt that by the beginning of this period it was of considerable significance as a determinant of the health of the British economy. An increasing number of people depended directly or indirectly on international trade for their livelihood. By the end of this period a quarter of the goods they produced were sold abroad and many of the other goods they manufactured were made from imported raw materials. Much of the food they consumed had been grown abroad and one-fifth of the goods they consumed came from abroad. So although it was a relatively small proportion of the total home production that was sold abroad, the idea of self-sufficiency had become more and more a myth, and the repercussions of fluctuations in the fortunes of British traders had a disproportionately powerful effect on the economy. The idea of the 'Great Depression' in the last quarter of the century was largely built on the evidence of trends apparently unfavourable to British traders, i.e. falling prices, a reduction in the rate of growth of the volume of exports, and stagnation in the total value of goods exported.

Although the prices of exports were falling, the prices of imports were falling even more rapidly, so that the terms of trade were moving in Britain's favour. Although exports were growing less rapidly than before, these would pay for a more than proportionate increase in imports. However the total value of imports rose by almost one-third in this period, and the deficit on the balance of trade reached £150m per annum by the end of the first decade of the twentieth century. The thesis of a Great Depression in Britain's trade in this period cannot be sustained. Although the economy was more dependent on trade than ever before, Britain was able to meet its main requirements from this sector, and pass on the benefits arising from the growing volume of trade which was essential for a higher standard of living.

Changes in the pattern of Britain's trade

The process of adaptation to the changing conditions of the late nineteenth century and early twentieth century involved considerable changes in the pattern of Britain's trade. There were marginal changes in the proportions of Britain's exports taken by the various markets. The growth of Europe's industries made it more difficult for Britain to sell her basic manufactures in that market, and the percentage of goods sold there declined from some 46 per cent in the 1860s to 38 per cent just prior to the First World War (B. R. Mitchell, *Abstract of British Historical Statistics*). However with the growth of purchasing power in Europe it is not surprising that it remained Britain's largest market. Germany and the U.S.A., Britain's biggest customers, had undergone comparatively rapid industrialization, and Britain's comparative cost advantage over these countries in the production of basic manufactures was whittled away. The early twentieth century saw the U.S. overhaul Britain as a producer of coal and iron, and by 1914 the U.S. and Germany preceded Britain as the foremost manufacturing countries in the world, while Sweden Russia, Canada and Japan had joined the ranks of industrial powers. However, much of this industrial production was for home consumption, and the proportion of Britain's exports going to the U.S. even increased slightly from 14 per cent in the 1860s to 15 per cent (1910–13), while Germany remained her second best customer until the war broke out.

Britain was able to take full advantage of her trade centres in Hong Kong and Singapore when the trade with Eastern Asia began to expand. China and Japan took an increasing proportion of Britain's exports, and Britain's special rights in Canton and other Chinese cities enabled her to reinforce a position where she supplied more of China's imports than all the rest of the world. Asia took 20 per cent of Britain's exports in the 1860s and over 21 per cent 1910–13. The increase in the share of exports going to Africa from 2 to 7 per cent in this period is accounted for largely by the growth of the South African market, although it also reflects the reciprocal nature of trade for Britain was buying more foodstuffs and raw materials from this continent. Britain continued to hold a market for about 10 per cent of her exports in the South American market despite competition from the U.S. and Germany.

The rate of increase of Britain's colonial trade in this period was relatively faster than in her other markets where problems of tariffs and developing home industries made it more difficult for Britain to sell her goods. About one-third of Britain's exports went to colonial markets at the end of the century compared with a quarter at the beginning of this period. The colonies had expanded their trade to supply about a quarter of Britain's growing import requirements in the years prior to the First World War. Traditionally Britain had performed the role of entrepôt to the colonies and other nations, so that these countries sent their goods to Britain and British traders re-exported these goods to other markets. The growth in the volume of world trade which made direct links worthwhile, and the navies built up by nations to carry this trade, brought about a steady reduction in Britain's role as an entrepôt. This was offset partly by the special services made available by the expertise of merchants and others in the City of London, and by the new commodities in world trade, especially raw materials and capital equipment, which were required in quantities often too small to make direct trade profitable. The proportion of re-exports in total exports fell from almost

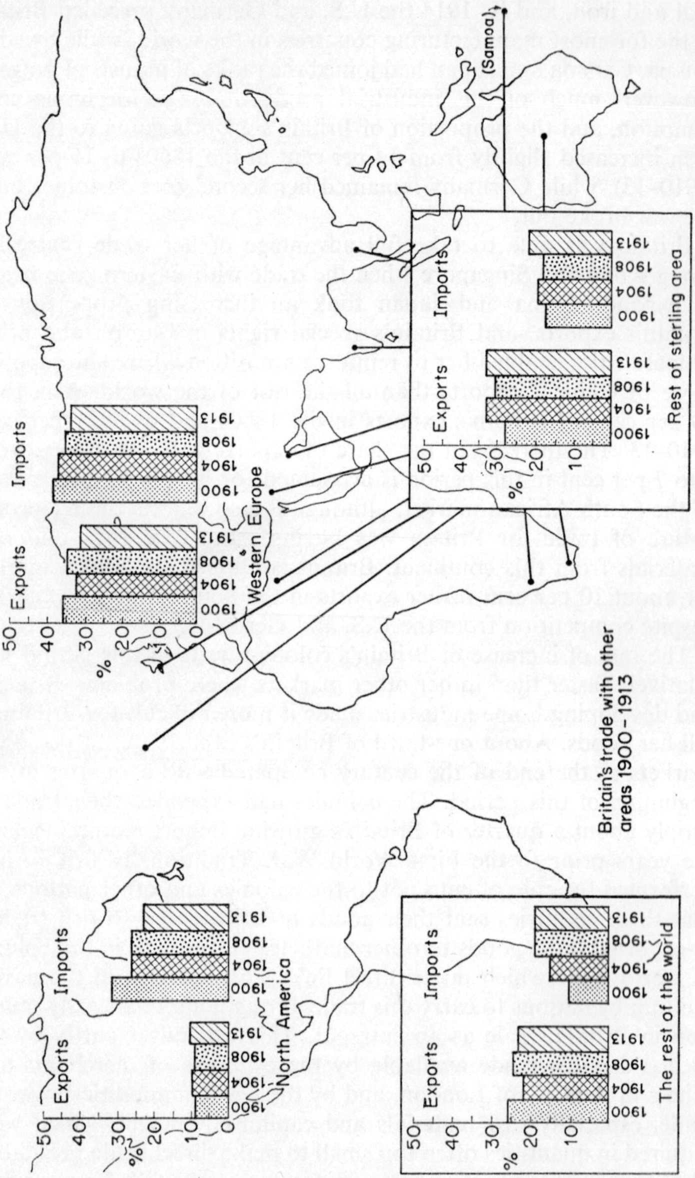
Western Europe
Exports
Imports
%
50
40
30
20
10
0
1900
1904
1908
1913
North America
Rest of sterling area
The rest of the world
(Samoa)
Britain's trade with other areas 1900 – 1913

one-fifth at the beginning of the period to one-sixth just before the war.

Exports

It was seen in the first chapter that Britain's exports were concentrated on a few basic manufactures. G. D. H. Cole has shown that over half of the exports in this period continued to come from the coal, iron and steel, engineering and textile sectors, and despite a trend towards greater diversity there seemed to be no real awakening to the fact that her comparative advantages in these basic products were fast disappearing. We have already seen that Britain's advantage now lay in the export of capital equipment and goods requiring high manufacturing skill. But there was no rush to transfer to this sector the factors of production from those industries, where the factors were not enjoying the innovations necessary to overcome the tendency towards rising costs. Readers will know that this *inherent* tendency is described in the Law of Diminishing Returns. The manufactured products which accounted for nine-tenths of Britain's exports at the beginning of the period formed only three-quarters of this trade in 1913. The relative importance of textiles had fallen to just under 40 per cent, while iron and steel maintained its 10 per cent, and capital goods increased their share from 5 to 10 per cent. The growing export of engineering products was a sound development, but the rapid rise in the share of coal until it accounted for almost one-tenth of Britain's exports in the immediate pre-war years meant that the heavy concentration on a few basic products remained a dominant feature of Britain's exports.

Imports

The spread of industrialization had its effects on the import side. Although foodstuffs and raw materials accounted for two-thirds of the total, with foodstuffs contributing a slightly larger proportion, the most dramatic development was the increase in the import of foreign manufactured goods so that in 1913 they amounted to one-fifth of total imports. About one-third of these manufactured items were required for furthering processing in Britain's major industries – iron and steel, engineering and chemicals. Most of these essential materials were imported from Europe and the U.S., although the British Empire territories contributed to the supplies of new basic materials – rubber, copper, crude oil – needed by Britain's industries. That Australia and New Zealand increased their share of Britain's imports, along with the United States and Canada, and South America (after it had recovered from a slump in its exports to Britain at the end of the nineteenth century) is due chiefly to the considerable increase in the amount of meat, dairy produce and grain imported. Although there was a decline during this period in the proportion of grain in foodstuffs imported, dairy produce increased from just over 10 per cent to more than 15 per cent, while meat imports accounted for over one-fifth of the total value in 1913 compared with less than one-twentieth at the beginning of this period. That Asia played no great part in the expanding sectors of Britain's import trade is demonstrated by the decline in the proportion it held from almost 30 per cent to just over half of that in 1913.

This chapter has been concerned with the process of adaptation to the changing conditions experienced by British traders in the period which took Britain from the mid-Victorian era of prosperity to the First World War. Although there are areas where change was slow to take effect, leaving Britain with a heavy concentration on basic exports, the adaptation was in general successful. The individual decisions made by the thousands engaged in trade, and influenced by such varying factors as the rising tariff walls, the opening up of new territories, the effects of earlier investment, the growing populations and the improvements in communications, enabled Britain to maintain its position high in the table of leading trading nations, although its proportion of the total of world trade fell from almost 20 per cent to less than 15 per cent in the period.

INVISIBLE ITEMS IN BRITAIN'S BALANCES 1868–1914

Shipping

We have seen earlier that Britain's comparative advantage in shipping had been growing since the third quarter of the nineteenth century as the introduction of first steam, and then iron, increased this advantage. Competition from the U.S. remained intense in the traditional lines, but the opening up of the Suez Canal in 1869 and the development of long distance trade routes gave an advantage to steam ships, which increased as their operating costs were halved by the end of the century, and technical improvements allowed larger loads to be carried. German competition in shipowning and shipbuilding was increasing by the end of the century, but in 1914 Britain still owned over one-third of the total tonnage of shipping in the world, which had more than doubled in this period. In 1914 the net earnings of Britain's merchant marine were over £90m, an increase by over half on the total at the beginning of the period.

Interest on Capital

The chief source of the increase in invisible earnings was the interest and dividends on capital invested with governments and private persons abroad. At the beginning of the period over half the loans went to European and U.S. governments (declining to a quarter by the end); with railways and similar enterprises taking another large part. In the early twentieth century Canada and India took over from Australia as the leading Empire borrowers, while the total of foreign investments increased from £700m to £2,400m in 1900, to about £4,000m in 1914. In 1913 the Empire accounted for half the total, while the U.S. with some 20 per cent, remained the largest single borrower, and railways, taking two-fifths of the total, was the most important single sector. Much of the investment followed the emigrants abroad and was dependent on a high rate of capital accumulation, and facilities for shipping abroad the real resources, particularly capital goods, implied in this foreign investment. A period of heavy investment in a market abroad was usually followed by an increase in British exports to that market. Trade fluctuations were paralleled by changes in the level of overseas investments, which was also affected by booms and slumps in the prices of the products of the borrowing nations. Britain's earnings from overseas investments almost quadrupled in this period, reaching £188m (*Imlah*) in 1914, (equal to one-fifth of Britain's total earnings from abroad), and much of this was reinvested abroad.

Financial services

At the beginning of the period earnings from insurance and from banking and other services were almost as large as those of the other great invisible earnings – shipping and overseas investments – but during this period they were left far behind, although they continued to grow slowly. The total value of these invisible earnings compared with the total value of Britain's visible export trade shows an increase from two-thirds to three-quarters in this period, having been as high as nine-tenths at one stage. Although Britain's expenditure on invisible items, like tourism and foreign investment in Britain, had increased slightly in this period the net effect of invisible items enabled Britain to pay for a considerable increase in the consumption of imported goods. The unfavourable balance of trade was turned into a favourable balance of payments on current account when invisible items were added and the surplus was reinvested abroad. While Britain had a surplus on the current account of the balance of payments its heavy capital investment overseas produced an unfavourable balance on the capital account equivalent to the current account surplus invested abroad. Ashworth points out that 'British import requirements became so vast and varied, the areas with profitable investment opportunities to attract a flow of British capital in excess of any reverse flow of dividends became so widespread, and the range of British export goods remained so limited that there were fewer and fewer countries to which Britain did not pay out more than it received in return'. To solve this problem Britain had to take multilateralism to its fullest extent, building up a huge surplus by exports to some countries, particularly in Asia, while those countries built a surplus through sales to other countries, particularly in Europe and America, while Britain satisfied her import needs largely from these countries. This system was highly vulnerable, but it proved flexible enough to carry Britain through the First World War.

SUMMARY

The trends which were summarized at the end of the first chapter in the main continued throughout this period 1867–1913, but a number of other developments became significant:

1. The proportion of goods produced in Britain that were sold abroad, and the proportion of foreign goods in the total consumed in Britain, increased considerably.

2. Although the volume of Britain's exports continued to increase rapidly the total value increased very slowly because the prices of exported goods were falling. Despite a favourable movement of the net barter terms of trade the value of imports increased.

3. The process of industrialization brought changes in the proportions of Britain's exports going to different markets. U.S. and German competition forcing Britain to take third place among the leading industrial nations, although these nations remained Britain's best customers, along with those in the British Empire.

4. Britain's exports remained concentrated on a few basic commodities, while textiles declined in importance and coal and engineer-

ing increased their shares. Re-exports declined as a percentage of total exports.

5. Manufactured items imported showed a striking increase although foodstuffs and raw material were far the most important sections, and meat, dairy produce and grain, the largest single items.

6. Europe and North America continued to be the main suppliers of Britain's imports despite the increase in the share of Empire countries, particularly Canada, Australia and New Zealand.

7. In the face of growing competition from first the U.S. and then Germany, and the growth of domestic navies, British shipping made a growing contribution to invisible earnings, and still accounted for one-third of the world's total tonnage in 1913.

8. Overseas investments was the fastest growing sector of the British economy and the main contributor to invisible earnings, accounting for one-fifth of Britain's total earnings from abroad.

9. The invisible earnings enabled Britain to turn a deficit of more than £150m per annum in the pre-war period into a surplus on the current account of the balance of payments, although heavy overseas investment somctimes produced a deficit on the capital account.

CHAPTER 3

BRITAIN'S TRADE BETWEEN THE WARS

THE EFFECT OF WAR ON TRADE

In the late Victorian period and early twentieth century those Britons who depended on international trade had been able to make superficial, but successful responses to the changes in international economic conditions. Britain had been able to maintain the health of an economy which was dependent to a large extent on her international transactions. But this had been done by patching the holes in the existing intricate system, which had proved flexible enough to enable the few basic commodities on which Britain's export trade was concentrated, along with the massive invisible earnings of shipping and overseas investment, to meet the growing need for imports with no great difficulty. The First World War exposed the vulnerability of this system when faced with the long-term dislocation of trade, and the fundamental changes in economic power which had been underway before the war began. The severe problems of the twenties and thirties arose partly from the strains of the war effort and post-war reconstruction, but mainly because earlier generations had been unwilling to make the fundamental changes in the directions of trade, the commodities in trade, and the nature of trade, while later generations were unable to produce the innovations which would give British traders the cost advantages over a wide range of products so essential to an effective export trade.

Exports

The dislocations caused by the war were predictable. Britain's exporters were cut off from some of the markets that had been doing well before the war; most obviously, those in Europe. Transport difficulties made it impossible to supply all the needs of other markets and notably Canada, South America, India and the Far East were forced to look to other sources to meet their needs, or to begin to manufacture the goods for themselves. Japan and the United States were quick to meet the needs we were unable to supply and to do this they increased their industrial production by three-quarters and one-fifth respectively. Britain was to find after the war that these nations could not be shaken out of her old and most valuable markets. The result was that Britain's total export trade declined more than 60 per cent in volume during the war period, although rapidly rising prices meant that the fall in the total value of exports was much less, remaining just over £500m (cf. £525m 1913). The effect of the decline in trade fell unevenly on industry; hardest hit was textiles which had been forced to reduce its output as a result of the difficulty in obtaining supplies. After the war the textile industry had to contend with the fall in demand in many of its traditional markets which now produced their own textiles or bought them from Japan. Other industries increased their capacity and expanded their output to meet wartime requirements. Munitions, shipbuilding, engineering and iron and steel all increased their productive capacity, but there was no increase in the export of their products, and the proportion of industrial production exported fell by 25 per cent during the war period. A wild optimism at the end of the war led them to have more plant constructed, but the expected boom in overseas demand was not forthcoming, and these industries too had to face the problem of excess capacity. This problem was accentuated because the efficiency of Britain's plant, even that which was newly constructed, was lower than the entirely new capital equipment which her competitors in Europe were forced to set up after their existing equipment had been destroyed in the war. The comparative cost advantage which had been disappearing since the turn of the century had gone for good in her staple exports. The trend towards rising costs was reinforced by the increase in fuel prices. The coal industry faced with the problem of expanding production to meet the needs of a wartime economy had used up the coal from the rich seams, so that in the post-war years only the less accessible seams remained and these were more costly to work.

Imports

The value of the pound at home was drastically reduced by the war-time inflation, and the main element in the rise in the general level of prices was the increasing cost of imports. Inevitably some of Britain's sources of essential supplies were cut off by the hostilities, while her needs were increased greatly by the demands of war. Other sources of supplies were available, but they were, of course, more costly, or they would have been exploited before. Britain's naval supremacy kept open for her far more channels of trade than were available to her enemies, but even so, essential materials were in short supply. The prices of imports increased more and more in the war period, and as the hazards of transporting them increased, so did the cost Germany waged a powerful U-boat campaign on shipping approaching Britain's shores, and essential food supplies were drastically cut. British farmers made every effort to increase home supplies, but much foodstuff had to be imported. With the rising price of imports and the increased needs of a wartime economy Britain's import bill soared drastically. The index of the total volume of imports shows an increase in the war period of less than one-third, but the value increased to more than one and a half times its previous level and in 1918 over £1,300m was spent on Britain's imports.

Invisibles

The financial and other services which had been built up in the country to be available to traders all over the world were much less effective invisible earners when the volume of world trade was diminishing, although British insurance found its business increasing as the risks of trade grew greater. But the London acceptance and discount houses were unable to recover the former volume of business in acceptance credits. Britain's other major invisible earnings, shipping and overseas investment, were both greatly affected by the war. Apart from the reduction in the amount of carrying to be done as trade diminished, there were fewer countries willing or able to use British ships to carry their goods. The entrepôt trade was the sector hardest hit, earning only £31m in 1918, less than one-third of its pre-war value. British shipowners experienced heavy losses particularly in the later part of the war: some 7 million tons representing 40 per cent of the merchant marine was lost in the four years. After the war Britain could not rely to the same extent as before on earnings from overseas investments to help to correct the balance of payments situation, although the invisible earnings were sufficient to keep the balance of payments on current accounts favourable until the heavy deficit in 1918 swamped all the surpluses of the early war years. The Government relied heavily on the expedient of overseas borrowing to maintain the allied armies' efforts. A sum approaching £2,000m was raised abroad to lend to the allies while over £1,300m was borrowed abroad for Britain's own purposes. From having been a large creditor in 1913 Britain had become, by 1918, a considerable debtor on the short-term capital account. Many of her long-term assets remained, of course, although over £500m's (almost one-tenth Britain's foreign assets) worth of privately owned overseas investments had been sold and her short-term credits run down. The hope that all these debts would be paid off in reparations from Germany proved unfounded. Britain was fortunate that sterling maintained its international exchange value at a time when many currencies were uncertain in value and depreciated by war needs, and there was no accepted world-wide monetary standard except for those countries like Britain that adhered to the Gold Standard. Britain's main currency problems stemmed from the shortage of dollars.

By 1918 the British economy had undergone the considerable adaptation that had been necessary to create an economy geared to the needs of wartime. All other considerations took second place to the need to keep Britain in the war even if it meant the wastage and destruction of the economic resources that would be vital to the post-war reconstruction. But the loss of manpower, of shipping and of other capital equipment was less severe than on the continent, and it was relatively unimportant when compared with the changes in economic forces brought about by the war. The loss of markets and of permanent international financial assets were but two of the symptoms of the changes. The United States had benefited from the changing economic position to take the role of the leading trading nation in the world and the leading international lender. Europe, which had been responsible for three-quarters of the world's trade, found that countries like Canada, Argentina, and Brazil which had previously been dependent for the supply of manufactured goods now produced many of their own. Not until 1929 did Europe again reach the level of manufacturing output which had been achieved in 1913. The post-war reconstruction was to be a difficult time.

THE POST-WAR PERIOD

The period immediately following the First World War was one of considerable instability as the transformation from a war economy to a peace economy took place all too rapidly. Soldiers returning home from the war found it difficult, if not impossible, to obtain jobs, and, after a period of boom as the consumer goods industries increased their production in anticipation of peacetime prosperity, the number of unemployed rose from 135,000 in 1917 to 448,000 in 1919 and to 2,540,000 in 1921. The industries producing for war needs quickly cut back their production: the output of steel falling from 9·72 million tons in 1917 to 7·89 million tons in 1919, and, after an increase in 1920, to 3·70 million tons in 1921, while the tonnage of shipping built, which had been maintained at a high level until 1920 when 2·4 million tons were constructed, fell to half a million tons in 1921. The short-term post-war boom of 1919–20 swung into the serious slump of 1921. From the low point of 1921 the economy experienced a recovery and the years from 1925 to 1929 were relatively prosperous, and apart from the year of the General Strike, 1926, there was an upward trend in the indices of industrial production which continues until 1930. It is significant that the exceptions to this general pattern occur in the industries which were most dependent on the export trade.

Reasons for the decline in Britain's Exports

In the early years of the twentieth century Britain's exports had been growing in volume at an average rate of more than 3 per cent per annum. During the war period they declined, and this decline continued up to 1929 at an average rate of 1·8 per cent per annum. In the years of the twentieth century prior to the First World War the growth in the volume of Britain's exports had been such that the average level of exports in the 7 years before the war was over 3 per cent higher than the average of the first 7 years of the century. But each succeeding period in the inter-war years showed a decline in the volume of exports: that of 1921–29 was 1·8 per cent down on 1914–21 and 1930–37 was 2·2 per cent down on 1921–29. In some years the record was better, as in 1929 when the volume reached the 1913 level, but after that the trade depression was severe. The return of the Gold Standard in 1925 (see pp. 29 and 36) at an overvalued exchange rate created added difficulties for Britain's exporters, who found themselves priced out of world markets. With the general level of prices above the 1913 level (1913 = 100, 1920 = 193, 1929 = 154, 1937 = 102), the effect of the fall in the volume of exports was less obvious before 1929, but the table on page 22 shows the dramatic fall after that year:

EXPORTS AND RE-EXPORTS IN £M (f.o.b.)

1919: 963	1924: 953	1929: 848	1934: 460
1920: 1569	1925: 940	1930: 666	1935: 536
1921: 822	1926: 790	1931: 461	1936: 520
1922: 836*	1927: 839	1932: 422	1937: 606
1923: 898	1928: 853	1933: 422	

* Change in the series. [See *Key Statistics*.]

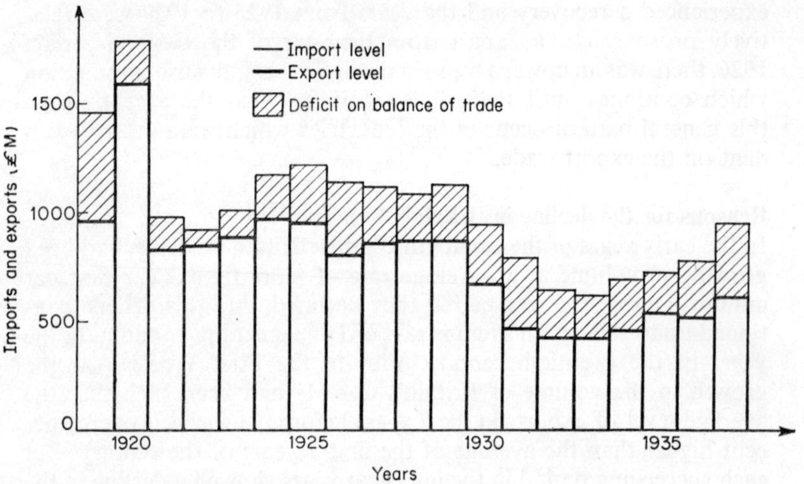

The decline in the level of exports of two basic commodities accounts for much of the fall in the general level. Although two-thirds of the exports of manufactures before the war belonged to groups which had a declining share in the inter-war period. The two basic commodities were cotton and coal, and in the pre-war years they supplied nearly two-fifths and one-tenth respectively of total exports. These industries were highly dependent on foreign markets, which took four-fifths of the total cotton output, and one-third of the coal output. Coal kept up its share of the declining export trade until after 1933 when it was still responsible for 12 per cent of the total. But the volume declined from over 60 million tons exported in 1924 to under 36 million tons in 1938. The explanation for the decline in the volume of coal exports is to be found in the opening up of coal deposits in other countries, and in the gradual replacement of coal by other fuels. Some ships were coming to be powered by oil-burning engines, or diesel motors, and the demand for coal for bunkering was, in consequence, falling. The value of cotton goods exported in 1933 was less than one-third of the 1924 level, but even then it represented 27 per cent of Britain's total exports.

Although there was stagnation and decline in world trade, Britain's export trade fared worse than that of most other countries, and the distribution of her export markets and the type of commodities her trade relied on so heavily, were responsible for this. In 1913 Britain exported over 13 per cent of the world's total, by 1927 her proportion was down to 11 per cent, in 1932 10 per cent, and in 1937 just over 9½ per cent. Britain sold almost three-quarters of these exports in the primary producing countries, and in doing so accounted for half of all European commodities sold outside that continent, while British exports represented only a quarter of all exports by European countries. Britain's share of the imports of all her major markets declined between 1913 and 1937 as the table below in which the countries are representative of each area of trade illustrates:

BRITAIN'S SHARE OF THE IMPORTS OF:

	1913	*1929*	*1937*
	%	%	%
U.S.A.	15	7	6
Germany (W. Europe)	8	6	5
India (Asia)	64	42	31
Australia (Australasia)	51	39	42
Argentine (S. America)	31	17	20
Sweden (Scandinavia)	24	17	19

Calculated from W. A. Lewis's *Economic Survey*.

The growing competition in the production and export of textiles from Japan and India was responsible for the decline of the Indian and Asiatic markets, while the enormous increase in the U.S. industrial capacity brought competition for U.K. goods in the South American markets. There was a steady increase in the proportion of Britain's exports going to Empire countries from just over one-third in the period 1909–13 to almost two-fifths 1919–26 and nearly half 1935–39. The value of this trade (not including Canada) had been £171m in 1913, rising to £303m in 1924, then falling to £149m in 1933, before rising to £222m in 1937. In the 1930s the African markets,

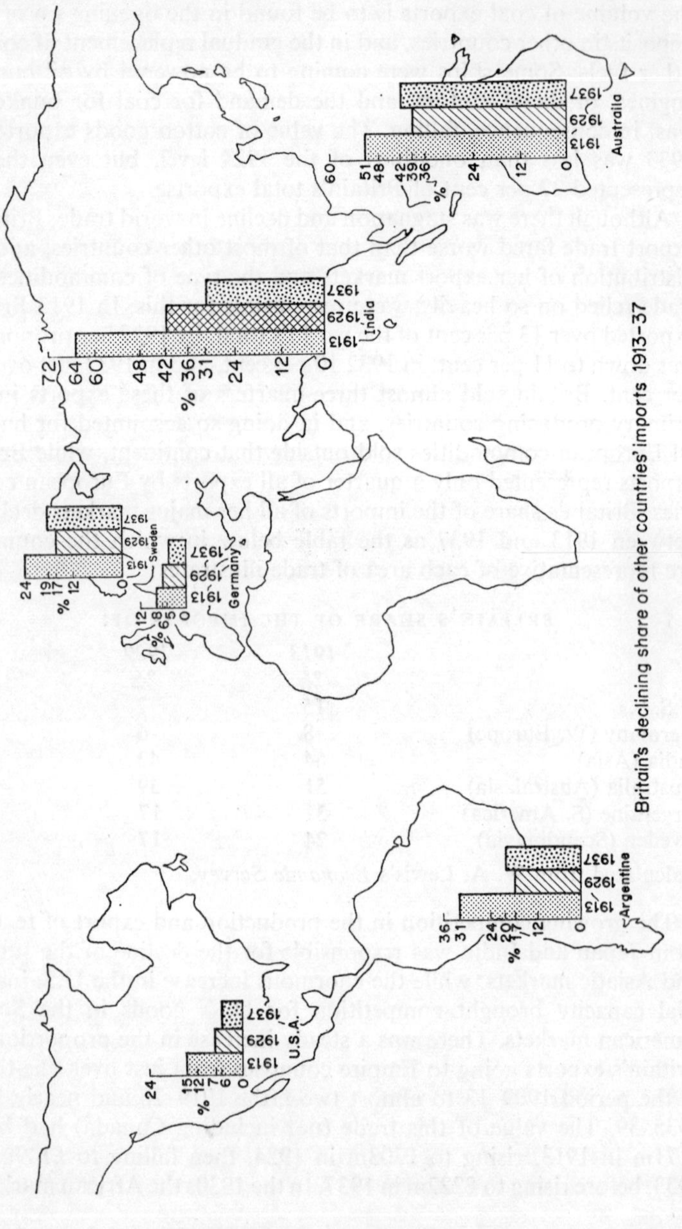

Britain's declining share of other countries' imports 1913–37

and especially the tropical British colonies, taking the simpler manufactures on which Britain concentrated, increased their share of Britain's exports to one-sixth of the total, to become as important as the Asian market. The other market to increase its share was Australasia, taking almost one-tenth of the total.

Britain was lagging behind the U.S. and Germany in exports of the new manufactures for which demand was growing. Machinery, chemicals and motor-cars were important growth sectors; but in Britain there is no significant increase in the output of chemicals before the 1930s, when Germany's output was twice, and the U.S. three times that of Britain. The value of chemicals exported in 1919 was £42m and in 1920 £58m. This was much higher than the value for any year until after the Second World War. The number of private cars produced increased rapidly from 106,000 in 1913 to 243,000 in 1921, to 981,000 in 1929, and to 1,984,000 in 1938, but at the beginning of the period cars and railway rolling stock accounted for not more than 2 per cent of Britain's total exports; while machinery, in which Britain's advantages were considerable, supplied less than 8 per cent. A whole new range of consumer goods had resulted from the new technology. Britain's mechanical, electrical and electronic engineering trades should have been capable of winning a major share of the world's markets for these goods, but the new type of goods required special knowledge and service from the traders, and in the "buyers market" of the inter-war years salesmanship, packing, delivery and after-sales service were becoming more important.

Imports

Britain's import trade follows a similar cyclical pattern to that of exports: the post-war boom 1919–20 is followed by a short-term slump 1921–22, before a period of relatively stable expenditure on imports, 1924–29, and then a more serious and long-term slump in the 1930s and a slight recovery prior to the Second World War.

£M IMPORTS (f.o.b.)

1913: 706	1923: 996	1928: 1086	1933: 618
1919: 1464	1924: 1164	1929: 1107	1934: 681
1920: 1749	1925: 1199	1930: 948	1935: 721
1921: 987	1926: 1129	1931: 784	1936: 780
1922: 913	1927: 1104	1932: 639	1937: 945

These figures illustrating the total value of Britain's import trade in the inter-war years do not show fully that the volume of imports was much higher during this period than before the war. There was a 3 per cent per annum growth rate of imports in the period 1921–29, compared with a growth rate of 1⅓ per cent 1908–13, and even in the early 30s imports were growing in volume at over 1 per cent (Lewis). The fall in prices of imported foodstuffs and basic materials was the main reason for the volume of imports increasing while the expenditure on these imports in the 1930s was well below the 1929 level. Britain's import bill for foodstuffs always came to less than £400m in 1932–36 compared with £529m in 1929, and although imports were at a low level in 1932, by 1936 they were well up to the 1929 level. Throughout the period almost half the total value of imports came from this item. The industrial depression in the 1930s was the main cause of a spectacular decline in the value (c.i.f.) of basic materials imported from £418m in 1925 to £162m in 1932, and although the volume increased from that year, the value was slow to rise so that in 1938 only £240m worth of basic materials were imported. The value of basic materials and fuels imported amounted to almost one-third of the total import bill. The fall in the prices of goods in these categories was largely responsible for the more rapid fall in import prices than in export prices. The net barter terms of trade in the table below show how Britain was able to pay for a greater quantity of imports with the same quantity of exports:

NET BARTER TERMS OF TRADE INDEX

1913 = 100

1907	*1913*	*1919*	*1921*	*1929*	*1932*	*1937*
97	100	106	130	127	124	138

There was a steady increase in the proportion of imported manufactured items in the total of imports. Britain was probably importing more of the products of the new technology than she was exporting, but the 'manufactures largely for further processing' – iron and steel, other metals, semi-finished items – continued to be much more important than finished manufactures. Even so, this latter category, which had only been one-third as great in value as semi-finished in 1913, was almost half as great again in 1938. The prices of manufactured items were also heavily hit by the depression and the trade never again, in the period, reached the total value of the period 1925–29, when expenditure on semi-finished goods imported was consistently over £200m and on finished products averaged over £80m. The respective totals for 1933 were £67m and £37m, and for

1937 £164m and £71m. Together they accounted for over one-sixth of the import bill.

During the inter-war years there was a decline in the re-export of imported articles. This continued a trend that had been in existence before the war. In 1913 re-exports were over £100m, and although they reached more than £200m in 1920, they were down to £87m in 1930, and £61m in 1938. By 1929 they had fallen to less than 10 per cent of total imports compared with 15 per cent in 1913.

The effect of invisible items on the balance of payments

The previous chapters have shown that Britain had long had a deficit on her trade balance, and the years of the twentieth century prior to the First World War had been no exception to the general pattern as the table below derived from Imlah's figures illustrates:

year	*£ms Deficit on Balance of visible Trade*	*Services (including insurance)*	*Net earnings of shipping*	*Earnings on International investment*	*Surplus available for re-investment abroad*
1900	169	53	66	104	36
1910	144	73	96	170	169
1911	123	74	96	177	200
1912	145	81	102	187	199
1913	140	84	108	200	225

In the inter-war years the size of the deficit on the balance of trade was much larger than before:

BALANCE OF TRADE £M

1919	*1924*	*1929*	*1931*	*1937*
£501m	£211m	£381m	£408m	£339m

Before the First World War the earnings of Britain's invisible exports (shown in the table above) had been much greater than the deficit on the balance of visible trade, so that there had been a considerable surplus available for reinvestment abroad. In the inter-war period these invisible earnings were difficult to maintain and in the 1930s were seldom large enough to cover the trade deficit:

INVISIBLE EARNINGS £M

1919	*1924*	*1929*	*1931*	*1937*
£372m	£252m	£362m	£218m	£283m

(figures for invisible exports including government transactions).

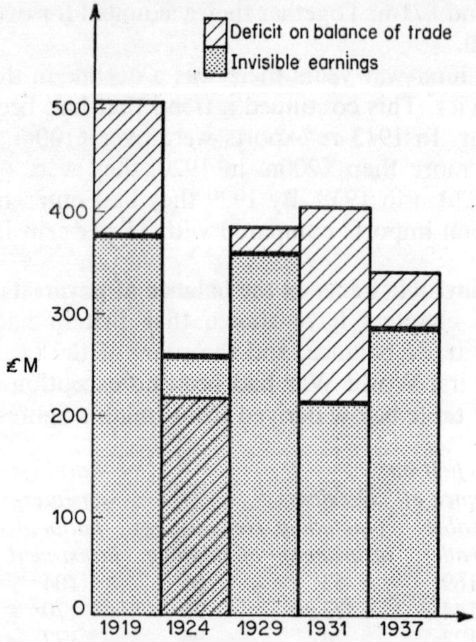

The British shipping interests soon restored the tonnage of shipping that had been lost in the war, but they were left with many ships built quickly for the emergency, which had a high running cost and were technically unsuitable for the cargoes of commodities newly entering world trade. The stagnation and decline of world trade meant that there was less carrying to be done, and as other nations built the fleets that were an essential part of national prestige the share of non British trade in the total trade carried by British ships fell from nearly one-quarter in 1910 to less than one-eighth in 1936. There was a small increase in the size of Britain's Merchant Marine up to 1931,

BRITISH SHIPPING (TONS)

1913	*1919*	*1925*	*1930*	*1935*	*1939*
19m tons	17m tons	19m tons	20m tons	17m tons	18m tons

but her share of the world shipping tonnage fell, although it remained remarkably high at 40 per cent in 1935 compared with 47 per cent in 1913. The earnings from British shipping failed to follow the rising trend which had characterized the pre-war period (see page 12).

SHIPPING EARNINGS £M

1913	*1924*	*1933*	*1937*	*1938*
£108m	£143m	£68m	£133m	£107m

The return to the Gold Standard

The services performed by the merchants and bankers of the City of London had for some time been important as earners of foreign currency, and in the pre-war years had steadily increased in importance (see pages 30 and 31). Insurance, discounting and accepting commercial bills of exchange, and the floating of foreign loans in London, had been the foremost of these services. The war, however, had dispersed many of the markets which had been centred on London, and there were now other markets for commodities, bullion, short-term bills and long-term bonds. The growth of New York as a financial centre was a blow to interests in the City of London. Moreover the decline in the surplus available for investment abroad, discussed below, and the impact of the war in reducing the level of capital accumulation in Britain, reduced the importance of London as a source of international funds. In a misguided attempt to restore her international financial reputation and win back her pre-war position of pre-eminence, Britain returned to the Gold Standard at the 1913 exchange level of £1 = \$4.87. The Bank of England was prepared to sell Gold at £4.2477 per oz. This rate soon proved far too high to be justified by Britain's trading performance – the costs and prices of her goods. The resultant pressure on Britain's reserves did nothing to restore confidence in this world trading currency. The situation was not improved by the absence of good order in the international money markets, which were unable to recover the settled conditions of pre-war years. The policy of expanding and depreciating currencies to pay for the debts accumulated in the war years, and the wildly fluctuating exchange rates as countries sought to find a level of prices in international markets which would make their exports competitive, did nothing to help to restore settled conditions. In these circumstances the countries which acted as the world's bankers had to keep larger reserves in order to meet the withdrawal demands which fluctuations in confidence were likely to produce. The policy of counteracting tendencies to withdraw funds by raising the rate of interest proved ineffective. But not only did the bankers keep larger contingency reserves but other countries which had previously kept reserves sufficient only for commercial purposes now kept reserves of foreign currencies as well as gold currencies. Thus Britain's gold and convertible currency reserves increased considerably, especially in the 1930s, and so did the sterling balances (see p. 63).

Year	*1913*	*1919*	*1922*	*1925*	*1927*	*1929*	*1930*	*1931*
Gold and convertible currency reserve £m	35	88	127	147	152	146	148	121

	1932	*1933*	*1935*	*1937*
Gold and convertible currency reserve £m	206	372	493	825
Sterling balances £m	468	538	600	808

Those countries which kept their reserves in the form of sterling balances in London generally followed the lead of sterling, rather than follow the dollar or remained linked to gold when G.B. left the Gold Standard. In 1931 they became a recognizable sterling bloc, and the term Sterling Area came to be used officially in 1940.

There was a decline in the total value of foreign issues floated in London, and, overall, Britain's earnings from these and the other 'invisibles' mentioned above, fell from over £80m in 1913, to just over £50m in the period 1929–33, and to just over £40m 1934–38.

The most important of Britain's invisible earnings were the dividends and interest which flowed in as a return on her overseas investment. We saw in the last chapter that Britain had been forced to realize some of her overseas investments to help to pay for the war (perhaps £500m), and with the heavy borrowing on behalf of her allies and on her own behalf (over £3,000m), Britain had become a debtor on short-term capital account in 1918. The new additions to Britain's investments overseas, amounting to just over £600m (1919–25), did little more than replace wartime losses but by 1927 the accumulated total had reached a new peak of over £4,250m. There was a decline from this peak to £3,750m in 1938. Although opportunities for overseas investment remained, indeed, some countries were crying out for capital, gone were the days of easily earned high yields in developing countries. The falling prices of their exported primary products and the increasingly complex and technical nature of products exported from the industrial nations made overseas investment in these countries either less profitable or more dependent on technical skill, so that for many the relative attraction of the safer home investment projects was greater. There was a decline in the interest and dividends received from abroad from almost £200m in 1913 to £150m in 1933, with a recovery to £185m in 1938. The increase in spending on foreign travel and in foreign investment in British projects must have cancelled out much of the increase in earnings from overseas investment.

With the increase in the size of the deficits on the balance of trade in the inter-war years, and the simultaneous decline in the invisible earnings which had previously been more than sufficient to meet the deficits, there was a fundamental change in the behaviour of the balance of payments on current account. A considerable deficit in 1918 and 1919 was converted to a large surplus 1920–23, before these surpluses decreased to a deficit in 1927; and then four more surplus accounts before the 1930s made the fundamental nature of the change clear with a run of deficits which was broken only in 1935. The surplus of Britain's invisible earnings was no longer growing fast enough to meet the enlarged deficit on visible trade year in year out. Britain was living on her capital.

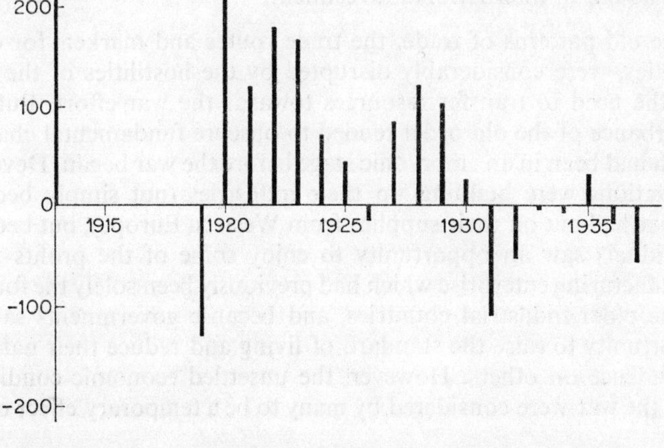

BRITAIN'S CURRENT BALANCE OF PAYMENTS *1913–37*

1913: +237	1923: +169	1928: +123	1933: 0
1919: −128	1924: + 72	1929: +103	1934: − 7
1920: +235	1925: + 46	1930: + 28	1935: +32
1921: +119	1926: − 15	1931: −104	1936: −18
1922: +173	1927: + 82	1932: − 51	1937: −56

(Key Statistics)

The causes of the changing pattern of trade in the inter-war years

There are two important questions to be answered: what brought about the stagnation in world trade in the inter-war years, and why did Britain fare worse than her rivals? The stagnation of world trade and the decline in the 1930s, has been ascribed to a variety of causes of which the most important are:

1. The disruptive effects of the First World War.
2. The need to make drastic adjustments to the structure of trade had been obscured in the pre-war period.
3. The decline in the volume of the trade in manufactures as a result of the slow adaptation of the old industrial countries to new products.
4. The tendency towards greater self-sufficiency.
5. Decline in the volume of the trade in primary products.
6. Decline in the demand of the primary producing areas as a result of a fall in their purchasing power.
7. The slowing down of the rate of population growth.
8. The general assumption of protectionist (high tariff) policies.
9. The chaos in international finance.
10. The fall in international investment.

The old patterns of trade, the trade routes and markets for commodities, were considerably disrupted by the hostilities of the war, and the need to transfer resources towards the war effort. But this disturbance of the old order tended to obscure fundamental changes which had been in an embryonic stage before the war began. Developing nations were building up their industries (not simply because the war had cut off their supplies from Western Europe), but because individuals saw an opportunity to enjoy some of the profits from manufacturing enterprise which had previously been solely the fortune of the older industrial countries, and because governments saw an opportunity to raise the standard of living and reduce their national dependence on others. However, the unsettled economic conditions after the war were considered by many to be a temporary effect of the earlier dislocation, and the drastic adjustments, so necessary if the older industrial countries were to meet the new conditions of world trade, were put off again and again as temporary expedients staved off threatened collapse.

The decline in the trade in manufactures was due largely to the fact that while the new technology brought new products on to the markets this did not compensate for the decline in the sales of the old products. The considerable growth of output in the manufacturing industries of the established industrial countries was the dynamic factor in the prosperity of these countries and the expansion of world trade in the half century before the First World War. The growth in the demand for primary products to meet the needs of these industrial countries had provided the developing primary producers with the purchasing power for buying manufactures. This mutually beneficial interaction had been reinforced by the reinvestment of payments surpluses by the industrial countries in the primary areas. The growth of the trade in manufactures was dependent on the growth of the purchasing power of the primary producers. The rates of growth of primary and industrial production are unquestionably linked, and it is probable that the decline in trade in manufactures was due not so much to the disruption caused by the war, nor very largely to the assumption of protectionist policies, and the development of home industries, but because the industrial countries were buying too little primary produce, and paying too low a price for these products. The poorer primary producing areas were forced to reduce their imports of manufactures, and they attempted to replace imported goods by the products of their home industries. The countries most dependent on direct trade with the primary producers suffered most. We have seen (p. 24) that Britain had a special relationship with these countries, selling a large part of her exports in their markets.

So Britain, in particular, suffered from the decline in demand for the old types of manufactured products. Coal was less in demand by her foreign customers and she was unable to make it more competitive with the new fuels because the industry was faced with rising costs. It is surprising that the contraction of output in the industry was very slow with 227 million tons mined in 1938 compared with 267 million tons in 1924. But slow adaptation to the unfavourable international economic conditions in the markets for the old export staples was a characteristic of the inter-war depression in Britain.

The United States, Russia, and Japan had taken the opportunity during the hostilities to establish a full range of manufactures for themselves and to develop the latest technical discoveries. They had wrested from Britain the industrial and commercial leadership of the world, but they failed to play the part that Britain had before the war in giving an impetus to world trade by their activities. Virtually the whole of Russia's manufacturing capacity (one-tenth of the world total in 1938) was employed in meeting domestic needs. Although the U.S.A. produced some 45 per cent of the world's manufacturing capacity in 1928 but a small proportion entered world trade because of the expanding home market. However it was the failure of the U.S. home market which set off the rapid downward slide to the world slump in the 1930s.

The new trends in industrialization had other adverse effects on Britain. The industries which the developing nations chose to establish first were often those which produced the commodities staple to Britain's export trade. Textiles predominated in Japan's industrial structure employing more than half her industrial workers. India and China, previously important British markets became net exporters of cotton goods. There was little compensation for Britain in this trend towards the products of the new technology. British industrialists were slow to see that the comparative cost advantages were moving into more highly processed goods, while Denmark, Sweden, Finland and the Netherlands seized the opportunity to increase their output of goods of this kind. However the international market for these goods was much narrower than the market for the old industrial staples. The inhabitants in the poorer primary producing regions found the motor-cars, electrical goods, electronic equipment, luxury consumer goods and the other new products far beyond their means. The inhabitants of the wealthier countries were, it is true, looking for new ways to spend their higher incomes, and their demand provided the basis for the development of the industries. But only the countries like the U.S.A. with a big domestic demand could produce on a large enough scale for economies to be reaped, and the price-range brought within the reach of a wide market. For international trade to develop there must be significant cost differences between the countries in the production of commodities. With the market for new industrial products virtually limited to the wealthier countries who manufactured the products the cost differences between these countries were not really significant. Some growth of trade in these products did take place, but other countries, like Britain, found they were spending about as much on the new products from other countries, as these countries were spending on their new products. It was to the potential growth sectors of machinery, equipment, transport, chemicals and durable household appliances that Britain should have looked more intensively for the opportunity to increase her exports. But there was no deliberate attempt to bring about the change from the old pattern of economic activities, or to transfer resources to these sectors.

The cumulative rate of increase in the world's population was lower in this period (less than 1 per cent) than it had been earlier in the century (1·5 per cent). The war was partly responsible for this, but the population grew fastest in the economically most prosperous regions. The standard of living in these regions was rising with increased productivity. So the increase in demand associated with a higher population was much less for the basic foodstuffs produced by the poorer primary producers than for luxury foodstuffs and manufactured goods. The food exporting countries found themselves producing more than they could profitably sell so that they were forced to reduce their prices. Their incomes from exports declined, reducing their ability to purchase manufactured imports, and balance of payments problems forced them back on their own resources.

The end of Free Trade

Faced with declining markets attempts were made to protect the home market for the products of home industries, and these protectionist policies further stifled world trade. The particularly severe deficit on the balance of payments coincided with the reversal of economic policy in Britain, although the agitation for a measure of protection supported by the Fair Trade League and others had been going on long before the end of the nineteenth century. The moves towards a policy of Imperial Preference had been underway since the Colonial Conference of 1897 and in March 1932 under the Import Duties Act, this came into force. The act imposed a general 10 per cent *ad valorem* tariff on most imports, including raw materials and foodstuffs. Most imported manufactured goods were subject to a 20 per cent duty, and some other goods including iron and steel paid an even higher duty. The series of agreements which followed immediately between Britain and Empire countries at the Ottawa Conference exempted Empire products, while these countries agreed to limit their industries' protection against British goods, and to have higher tariffs against countries other than Britain.

Britain made *ad hoc* bilateral agreements with seventeen non-Commonwealth countries including Argentine, Denmark, Sweden and the Baltic countries. They were required to increase the proportion of their imports which they bought from Britain. These measures did little to alter Britain's economic situation while they assisted the downward trend in the volume of world trade. Foreign competition for British goods was deflected away from Britain's stronger markets to areas where her hold was less strong; and the loss in unprotected market more than balanced the gain in the protected market. Britain's bilateralism was an obstacle to trade growth and had deflationary consequences.

Britain was also partly responsible for the chaos in international finance. The international monetary standards which had been generally accepted before the war, now came under fire from all quarters. In Britain the restoration of the gold standard in 1925 was regarded as a panacea for declining trade and investment overseas, as it was expected to set going a series of correctives, leading to a fall in prices which would correct the original disequilibrium in the balance of payments. It was regarded as essential for the re-establishment of Britain's position as the world's banker. In fact the restoration hampered the export staples – coal and textiles – because it put the prices of British goods well above those of her competitors, hindering competition in the old markets and restricting the development of new markets. The heavy deficit on the balance of payments forced Britain to produce measures which made international co-operation more difficult. Britain left the gold standard in the unilateral devaluation of 1931, but any gains were short lived as the U.S.A. followed in 1933 and France in 1936. With the depreciation of some currencies, and other currencies hit by hyper-inflation, with wildly fluctuating exchange rates and severe balance of payments problems, conditions were not conducive to the expansion of trade and investment overseas. Neither was London likely to enhance its position as the premier centre of international finance while British policies suggested such financial insecurity.

The political and social conditions, which had been so kind to overseas investment before the war, were no longer sympathetic. There were opportunities for good returns for the demand for investment capital was still high. But as the degree of risk increased along with the need for technical expertise, so investors looked on home investment projects more favourably. This tendency was reinforced in Britain by a decline in the level of private savings and the absence of a regular surplus on international transactions available for re-investment abroad.

The depressed conditions of world trade in the inter-war years can therefore be ascribed to a variety of causes, and the failure of Britain and other countries to arrest the plunge of the trade cycle was due partly to the lack of international economic co-operation, and partly to the failure to make drastic adjustments to the changing economic conditions.

SUMMARY

A. The war period

1. War-time inflation and the restriction of supplies led to a large increase in the value of imports, although the volume increased less. The volume of exports declined, but the value remained much the same.

2. The ability to meet the deficit on the balance of trade with an even greater surplus on invisible items was impaired by:

(*a*) heavy borrowing to cover costs of war;
(*b*) loss of shipping and carrying trade;
(*c*) instability in international monetary dealings;
(*d*) London's slowness in re-establishing itself as the centre of international finance.

3. The dislocations of war accelerated the trend in many of Britain's markets away from British goods to goods produced at home or in near-by, newly industrialized countries.

4. Britain's failure to make fundamental changes in the pattern of her trade prior to the First World War was largely responsible for the serious difficulties which arose in the inter-war years.

B. The inter-war period

1. Britain's exports suffered more than other industrialized countries because of:

(*a*) the distribution of her export markets, e.g. primary producers important British customers;
(*b*) the type of commodities exported, e.g. decline in demand for coal;
(*c*) increased competition from Japan and U.S.A.;
(*d*) Return to the Gold Standard.

2. Unemployment rose steeply after a short boom.

3. Post-war imports rose at a faster rate than pre-war imports, especially the manufactured items.

4. The pre-war decline in the re-export of imported articles continued.

5. The stagnation in world trade was the result of:

(*a*) the tendency to attempt greater self-sufficiency;
(*b*) the slowing down of the rate of population growth;
(*c*) high tariff policies;
(*d*) depreciation of some currencies, wildly fluctuating exchange rates, which affected confidence in world currencies;
(*e*) the slow adaptation of the old industrial countries to the production of new commodities for export.

CHAPTER 4

THE SECOND WORLD WAR AND ITS AFTERMATH

In 1938 the total value of U.K. exports was £471m + re-exports £61m. By 1948 many of the dislocations of trade which go with a major war had eased. The total value of U.K. exports was £1,582m + re-exports £65m. By 1958 the total value of exports and re-exports had increased to £3,250m + £141m, while in 1968 it is estimated that the total will exceed £6,000m. The trends in the total value of imports taken for each decade since 1938 are very similar: 1938 = £920m, 1948 = £2,078m, 1958 = £3,833m, 1968 estimated at more than £7,000m. The deficit in the balance of trade which appears throughout this period increased considerably in the last decade and was a major factor in the fundamental disequilibrium of Britain's balance of payments. A more detailed examination of Britain's overseas trade in each of these decades shows how this position came about.

1938–1948: THE PROBLEMS OF A WARTIME ECONOMY

The ability of the British island economy to obtain the imports essential for survival probably depended more on military than on economic factors. That is not to say that inability to pay for the things Britain required from abroad, or the refusal of overseas suppliers to accept sterling, would not have been disastrous, but in the event Britain was able to pay for her imports, although this meant an increase in her external debt by more than £3,000m, a reduction in her gold reserves by £150m (they had been £450m in 1938), and the sale of more than £1,000m of Britain's capital assets abroad (the value of these in 1938 was approximately £3,000m). The introduction of Lend-Lease in 1941 by the U.S.A. considerably eased the burden on Britain. By 1943 the U.S.A. provided a quarter of the armaments of British and Empire forces. With the support of the British Empire, the U.S., and other countries, there was no great danger of the sources of Britain's supplies drying up. But the task of transporting these goods to Britain proved extremely hazardous – though the supplies problem was never as acute as during the all-out German U-boat attack of the First World War. The Battle of Britain denied the Germans the air superiority which could have menaced the British supply routes. The main threat to the sea routes came from the U-boats and surface raiders and even the carefully developed convoy system, first introduced by Lloyd George in the First World War could not prevent severe losses to the mercantile marine, and ships were diverted from military use to make up for these losses. Britain's survival owes much to the brave efforts of the merchant-men who struggled across the Atlantic and from all parts of the world with essential supplies. Even so the fall in the volume of imports and exports was greater than at any time in the century we are covering. The average value of imports (at 1948 c.i.f. prices) for the 3 years 1935–38 had been more than £2,500m, and this had fallen to less than £2,000m for the 3 years 1946–49. Imports of food fell by a third, materials by a quarter, manufactures by two-fifths. Britain's exports fell more heavily, by 1941 they were at a half of the 1938 level and by 1944 at a third. The fall in exports was inevitable in an economy in which everything was sacrificed to the war effort. Those industries which were not directly geared to war requirements were pruned of labour and capital. The contraction of these industries, some of which were important exporters like textiles, and the expansion of agriculture, engineering, metals and fuels, was essential to meet wartime needs. The transfer of factors to the essential industries was not an easy operation especially where men and capital were highly specialized. So that it is remarkable that these industries managed to double their output in the first two years of the war in the face of a chronic labour shortage and high structural unemployment (nearly 1 million late in 1940). The labour which was available was unsuited to meeting the particular skills required. Some export trades suffered from recurrent shortages of raw materials and semi-manufactured products, but the production of essential war industries was seldom hampered in this way. The U.S.A., for instance, helped to meet the increasing British demand for the machine tools needed by munitions, transport and general engineering industries.

'Import substitution' and the fall in imports

Some 'import substitution' resulted from the growth of the war industries, particularly in agriculture where the Government encouraged production by grants, subsidies and guarantees. There was a relative fall in the price of home-produced food as compared with imported food. Britain's farmers increased their output by almost a half, supplying foodstuffs that had previously been purchased abroad. But this only partly explains the fall in expenditure on imported foods. The rise in the prices of foodstuffs, both home-produced and imported, and the introduction of rationing and import controls, brought a reduction of consumption by more than 5 per cent. Rationing played an important part in closing the gap between consumption and demand. The general rise in the level of prices without a corresponding rise in incomes meant that consumers had less money to spend on goods and services, imported or home-produced. This meant there was an adverse trend in the standard of living.

The substitution of home-produced commodities for imports is less important in the 'materials' category – for there are few adequate home-produced substitutes for ores, raw cotton, wool, timber and rubber. The decline of imports of raw cotton and wool was as much the result, as the cause, of the cut-back in the production of these industries which had become geared to the domestic rather than the export market. Much of the increase of home-produced materials substituted for imports consisted of scrap and waste products. Strenuous efforts by government authorities to develop habits of economy and to requisition metal of all sorts – even garden railings and fences – provided some part of the increased supply while controls brought a reduction in the export of materials. Improvements in technique and increases in productivity were further factors in the fall in the ratio of imported materials to industrial output. The index of industrial production increased from 100 in 1938 to 108 in 1948, while the index of the consumption of materials fell from 100 to 90 and the imported materials from 100 to 74.

The increase in oil imports is the main element in the increase in fuel imports in this decade. Home consumption of coal and oil increased by almost 10 per cent in this decade, to meet the needs of wartime industry, but part of the increased consumption was met by a transfer of coal from the export to the domestic market. The massive increase in the production of manufactured goods in Britain in the war period partly explains the greatest fall of any category of imports;

'manufactured' imports were almost halved. Government subsidies to home producers made the prices of home-produced goods more attractive than the prices of imported goods, while Government controls restricted the import of luxury goods. Undoubtedly the level of imports at the end of the decade was substantially below the level of free demand for them.

Britain's commitment to the war effort left but a small proportion of her resources for the export trade. Many of Britain's traditional customers looked to other sources for their requirements as South America looked to the United States, or they built up their own industries, accelerating the process which had been developing in the inter-war years. Difficulties in obtaining materials restricted the production of export industries and there were strong American objections to the use of materials made available cheaply under Lend-Lease arrangements being used in British exports which might be sold in competition with similar American exports. Under these arrangements Britain received some £7,000m worth of goods from the U.S. while she exported less than £2,000m worth to that country. Early in the war U.S. insistence that all goods Britain purchased had to be paid for had depleted Britain of dollars and gold reserves, but through Lend-Lease the United States helped Britain over the problem.

By 1943, following the entry of the U.S. into the war and the build-up of U.S. troops in Britain, the gold and dollar reserves began to rise with the U.S. expenditure to support their troops – an invisible export for Britain. As a result the range of goods and materials available under the Lend-Lease was restricted. Americans did not see why Britain should build up reserves and enjoy Lend-Lease facilities. But by 1944 the U.S. administration recognized that it was important for Britain to build up reserves for reconstruction when the war was over, and no longer insisted on restrictions on Britain's exports. This did not, however, solve Britain's problem of how to obtain dollars, and this was the major preoccupation of the immediate post-war years.

A detailed examination of this decade 1938–48 is limited by the scarcity of information regarding the imports and exports of the war period. That there was a sudden drop in the volume of imports and a much steeper fall in the volume of exports there can be no doubt. The deficit in the balance of visible trade which had been about £300m in 1938 undoubtedly increased, and if we assume a price level of imports and exports at about double the pre-war level, the deficit was perhaps £650m in 1946. The increase in Government expenditure abroad, to some £300m in 1946, and the reduction in income from invisible items to perhaps half of its pre-war level helped to accentuate the balance of payments problem.

Attempts to ameliorate problems of international liquidity at the end of the war

Towards the end of the war efforts began to be made to deal with the international monetary and trading problems which were likely to threaten the post-war world. Even in 1942, the U.S. had wanted the U.K. and the allies to prepare for the elimination of discriminatory treatment in overseas trade and for the reduction in tariffs and other trade barriers. Britain was forced to accept this policy, which was certain to favour the economically more powerful Americans, as part of the Lend-Lease agreement. In fact little progress was made in this decade, and even the setting up of the General Agreement on Tariffs and Trade in 1947 and the signing of the Havana Charter by over 50 countries had little effect until the next decade. 'When Europe emerged from the war, its network of quotas and special accounts and bilateral treaties regulating them still enmeshed its foreign trade and financial relations across frontiers' (Postan).

This problem of international liquidity, and in particular the acute shortage of dollars, was in the event, the most serious difficulty to be faced in the immediate post-war years. John Maynard Keynes had suggested a new international money of account with overdraft facilities (cf. Special Drawing Rights), but this was not acceptable to the Americans. The Bretton Woods Conference in the U.S.A. was attended by most of the trading nations of the free world and it proposed to set up an International Monetary Fund (see below) whose main function was to make more readily available a supply of currencies acceptable internationally for the finance of trade. If the volume of world trade was to recover after the war this supply of money was essential. Britain was pressed into ratifying the Bretton Woods Agreement in return for a Dollar Loan of almost $5,000m. The loan was made necessary by the sudden end of Lend-Lease in August 1945, by the need to replace Lend-Lease supplies with imports of fuel, raw materials and food obtainable only in the dollar area, for with the population growing and industries expanding imports could not be cut back, by the poor performance of the Sterling Area in exporting to the Dollar Area and by the resulting balance of payments crisis. The U.S. loan was supplemented by a Canadian loan of $1,250m on rather more generous terms.

The International Monetary Fund

In the post-war years many countries were short of the currencies which were essential if they were to participate in international trade. It was this shortage of generally acceptable means of settling international debts arising out of trade and other transactions which exercised the Governments and their economists at this time. As a result of the Bretton Wood Agreements of 1944, a Special Agency of the United Nations, the International Monetary Fund, was set up in 1945. It aimed to facilitate exchange procedures among its members, and to set up a multilateral payments system for this purpose. It was dedicated towards the removal of unnecessary restrictions on foreign exchange that might hamper international trade. It was intended to be 'an international bank holding a generally acceptable currency, (*which*) could provide the initial liquidity on which could be built a superstructure of mutual obligations that could carry a much higher level of international trade on the basis of similar national resources' (Pollard).

The main function of the I.M.F. has been to provide short-term financial aid to member countries which were in balance of payments difficulties, usually by providing the countries with the currencies of which they are short, in exchange for deposits of the member's own currency. By 1960 there were over 80 member countries paying a quota which determined their voting rights; 25 per cent of the quota was to be paid in gold, and the rest in the member's own currency. Limitations were placed on the drawing rights of the members in other currencies.

It was intended that pressure should be brought against a member country that was persistently in a favourable balance of payments situation for if any currency in the Fund was used up and no more paid in, there should be discrimination against that country by the other members. However the I.M.F. had little success in this direction in the early years. The Fund of $7 billion consisted largely of 'soft' currencies and was far too small to meet the shortages of dollars and other 'hard' currencies arising out of the considerable imbalance in trade and payments between the dollar area and the rest of the world. This imbalance resulted from demands for goods and services available only in the Dollar Area which boosted U.S. exports while the U.S. neither allowed imports in freely, nor invested her surpluses abroad at this time. Unless they obtained special permission countries could use only a quarter of their quota to the Fund, and borrowing did not prove easy. The assumption of the

Conference that within a short time restrictions and controls on trade and payments could be removed, and the maintenance of equilibrium in international trade left to the normal workings of the price mechanism was seen, before the end of this decade, to be a dream. Equally unrealistic was the attempt of the Conference to force Britain to restore the full convertibility of the Sterling Area before the end of 1947. Limited convertibility was indeed attempted, but by August of that year the attempt was brought to an end as dollars were rapidly drained away. Britain's efforts to deal with the dollar crisis will be discussed later.

The International Bank for Reconstruction and Development

The establishment of the I.M.F. and the attempted restoration of convertibility was part of a widespread effort to put world trade back on its feet after the war. The effort was spearheaded by the U.S. at the Bretton Wood Conference. The International Bank for Reconstruction and Development (the World Bank) was another institution born at the Conference in 1945. It was designed to undertake international investment, but it started very slowly lending only $800m in its first 6 years, partly because of the lack of funds, partly because of its policy of extreme caution in making loans and the need to build up a contingency reserve. Britain could give little support at this time, as she was mainly concerned with investing in colonial reconstruction – the Colonial Development Corporation was set up for this purpose in 1948 – and in development and in paying off some of the sterling balances accumulated in the war. With the memory of the depression in trade which followed the First World War, the I.B.R.D. was expected to counter trends towards trade depression with widespread lending, but its resources were far too limited. This function was much more effectively carried out by Marshall Aid (see below p. 48).

The General Agreement on Tariffs and Trade

The progressive liberalization of international trade was another part of the policy for post-war reconstruction, and we have seen that G.A.T.T. was set up for this purpose at the Geneva Conference in 1947. Although the framework of trade agreements in G.A.T.T. was intended as the half-way stage to a permanent International Trade Organization, it was G.A.T.T. which became permanent with three main aims:

1. To ensure full employment in the member countries and raise their standards of living.

2. To expand production and the exchange of goods.

3. To promote the progressive development of the economies of contracting parties. The official statement declares that the contracting parties are 'desirous of contributing to these objectives by entering into reciprocal and mutually advantageous arrangements directed towards the substantial reduction of tariffs and other barriers to trade, and to the elimination of discriminatory treatment in International Trade'. The only acceptable protection was to be tariffs resulting from multilateral negotiations.

The Americans did not succeed in clearing away all forms of discrimination against them, some preferential treatment for 'development purposes' remained, and certain quantitative controls were allowed to deal with serious balance of payment problems. It was the fundamental imbalance in world trade which prevented G.A.T.T. from achieving much in its early years; even so a series of negotiations for general tariff reductions were begun, and the liberalization of international trade was partly due to this. Britain was unable to play a leading part because of the lack of success in her export drive, the loss of invisible earnings and her huge demand for dollar imports made protection and discrimination inevitable if serious balance of payments crises were to be avoided.

In the attempt to restore her international trading position after the war, Britain's exporters were given priority for materials, manpower and shipping and they were aided by interest rates which were kept artificially low to encourage production. But by 1945 exports had fallen to little more than a third of the 1938 level, receipts from exports were only £800m of which £450m was in non-recurring items, while imports were almost £2,000m, and the Government set a target for exports to reach 175 per cent of the 1938 level, in an 'export drive'.

The export drive

In 1946 with favourable market conditions in Africa and India, and with Western Europe restocking in a mild post-war boom, and with a consumer boom in the U.S., the exporters enjoyed some success; the value of exports reaching £70m per month in the first half year and totalling £915m for the whole year. But the import content of these exports drove up the bill for these materials, while rising import prices caused a deterioration in the terms of trade and the Coal Crisis of 1947 cost Britain perhaps £200m of exports, so that in 1947 payments were again heavily in deficit to the tune of £381m.

The invisible earnings, which in the past had done so much to convert the unfavourable balance of trade into a favourable balance of payments, had declined steeply. The total earnings of shipping were down by more than 30 per cent. Over a quarter of Britain's overseas investments had been sold off while the overseas debt had been increased by a rise in the sterling balances to more than £3,350m and the need to repay this and to promote development in colonial territories was a severe strain on the U.K. payments, which was accentuated by the rapid outflow of dollars, with the attempted convertibility, as holders of sterling balances especially in European countries lost faith in the pound. Agreements had to be made with India, Pakistan and Egypt, the largest holders of sterling balances to limit the rate at which the balances could be converted into dollars. The attempted convertibility resulted in Britain losing almost £1,000m in gold and dollar reserves. By the end of 1947 less than £2,500m remained.

Cyclical trends of the mid-Twentieth Century

The year 1948 was in some ways a turning point, though Britain's trade was beginning to change even before this decade began. Total exports had increased from just over £900m in 1946 to more than £1,600m in 1948, and the deficit of over £400m on the balance of visible trade in 1947 had been reduced to less than £200m, and with the recovery of her invisible earnings (contributing more than £250m, apart from Government expenditure) the balance of payments on the current account showed a surplus for the first time since the beginning of the war. The average annual growth rate of Britain's exports for the 20 years after 1948 (1·7 per cent) has been much greater than that for the 30 years before 1948 (0·2 per cent). Even so it was much lower than the growth rates enjoyed by many other European countries: Germany more than 16 per cent p.a., Italy more than 12 per cent, Netherlands more than 10 per cent and France almost 8 per cent. In the period 1948 to 1968 the total value of exports from Western Europe has almost quadrupled (U.N.O. Economic Bulletin for Europe). The trade of the O.E.C.D. countries of Western Europe has indeed been growing faster than that of any other part of the world. Trade between O.E.C.D. countries has been growing half as fast again as trade between Eastern Europe and other countries.

World trade has just about doubled in value in this period, 1948–68. Perhaps the main explanation for the growth of Britain's export trade after 1948 is that she was merely sharing in a world trade growing faster than ever before.

Marshall Aid

The introduction of Marshall Aid in April 1948 played an important part in the recovery of Western Europe. More than $17,000m flowed into Europe in the next 4 years to help to overcome the dollar crisis. A measure of European co-operation was made a prerequisite by General Marshall and this led to the formation of the European Payment Union whose function was to arrange for the allocation of aid, for mutual credits among members, for the interchangeability of members' currencies and for the clearing of financial claims arising out of current trade. In the process of settlement it automatically created some short-term credit for member nations. Here was another institution pledged to the liberalization of trade and payments, and aiming also to raise the standard of living in Europe through increased productivity. Trade was freed from the worst of the restrictions and shortages, but the free movement of capital could not come about until international development brought a better distribution of reserves of gold and foreign currencies with a flow of funds from the U.S. to Europe. Pollard has described this Aid Programme of the Truman Administration as 'a scheme of aid entirely without precedent in the history of the world, generous to a degree, visionary and yet practical, not devoid of political considerations, and yet an act of philanthropy more than of self interest'. Along with the American military expenditure and investments more than £25,000m left the U.S. for Europe before the end of the decade.

Events leading to devaluation

But even after 1948 Britain was not yet out of the wood. Personal expenditure on consumption goods had been allowed to rise, and severe import restrictions were necessary to prevent these growing too rapidly, even though exporters were enjoying boom conditions abroad. The import bill was rising, but there had been a transfer to non-dollar sources for most of this increase, while the export drive to the U.S. had begun to take effect with an increase from £92m in 1947 to £136m in the value of exports. However the dollar bill for imports was £408m in 1948 and the dollar deficit was a continued anxiety, for the reserves were continually under pressure and at no time in this decade were they large enough for Britain to be able to face with confidence even small changes in the prices of British goods, or in the level of activity in the economy or in the willingness of foreigners to hold sterling. In particular a threatened deficit in the balance of payments brought a hasty series of restrictive measures to protect the scanty reserves (shown below):

	Gold Reserves	*I.M.F Drawing Rights*		*Gold Reserves*	*I.M.F. Drawing Rights*
	£m	*£m*		*£m*	*£m*
1948	457	(308)	1953	899	(509)
1949	603	(444)	1954	986	(549)
1950	1178	(443)	1955	757	(549)
1951	834	(453)	1956	799	(347)
1952	659	(453)	1957	812	(345)

Some further defence was provided by unused I.M.F. drawing rights (in brackets above).

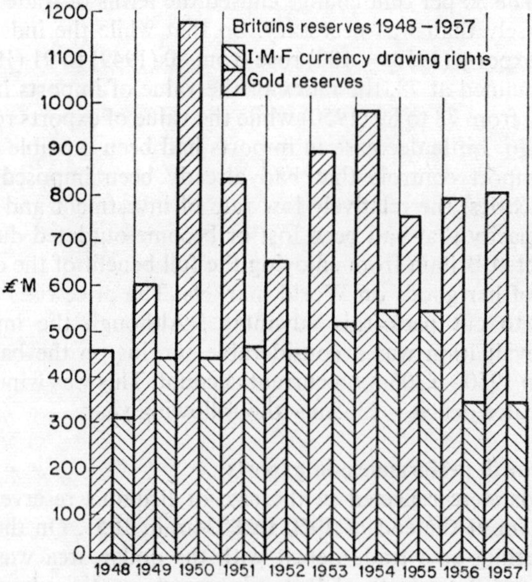

The boom in the U.S. did not continue in 1949 and the value of U.S. imports fell by 7 per cent. British exporters were finding U.S. markets more competitive. At the same time the growth of home demand was providing an easy alternative market. With the trend back towards an unfavourable balance of payments pressure on the pound mounted. The Government hesitated to take action and it was not until September 1949 that Sir Stafford Cripps announced a devaluation of sterling from £1 = $4.03 to $2.80 – more than a 30 per cent reduction. Britain was not alone, Italy followed with an 8 per cent reduction, Belgium 13 per cent and Germany 20 per cent.

Effects of devaluation

The economic prestige of the Government which was recovering from the attempt at the convertibility of sterling was sent staggering by the poor timing of this devaluation. 'It marked the failure of the Government's economic policy' (Pollard). The rise in the cost of living, a round of wage demands, the end of price control, a cut-back in the social welfare programme were inevitable repercussions. And the devaluation was by no means the end of the international trading problems. The 30 per cent change caused the terms of trade to move more adversely than was necessary. So that while the index of the volume of exports (1958 = 100) rose from 80 (1949) to 91 (1950) and imports remained at 78, the index of the value of imports increased enormously from 78 to 89 (1950) while the value of exports rose from 71 to only 76. Little decrease in imports had been possible with the range of import controls that had already been imposed. In the export industries, the relatively low rate of investment and replacement of capacity that had been lost or become outdated during the war, prevented Britain from enjoying the full benefit of the competitive prices of her goods on World markets. The price rises at home were soon to cut back this advantage. Although the immediate effect of devaluation was a considerable surplus on the balance of payments in 1950 – £306m on current account. This was wiped out in an even greater deficit – £365m – the following year.

Britain's growth performance in exports

These trends were reflected in the size of Britain's reserves falling from £1,178m at the end of 1950 to £834m in 1951. On the benefit side the sterling area trade deficit with the dollar area was almost wiped out and the growth of Britain's exports continued apace, but now the added difficulty of the Korean War which had broken out in June 1950 had to be faced and 1951 saw the end of a most successful export drive, the value of exports having more than doubled between 1946 and 1951. All the main classes of exports enjoyed a share of this growth. The value of manufactures exported increased from less than £800m to more than £2,000m. Textiles trebled their export earnings to £470m, more than 5 times their 1938 value. A less rapid growth occurred in Metals which doubled its export value to £265m in 1951. Perhaps the most important increase was that of machinery and transport equipment which earned nearly £900m for Britain in 1951 compared with less than £300m in 1946. Chemicals was another fast growing sector exporting £193m worth in 1951 (£80m 1946).

This growth performance of Britain's exports occurred because of the concentration of exporters on the growth sectors of world trade. Some 65 per cent of the commodities exported enjoyed expanding markets, and only 30 per cent were struggling in declining markets. As a larger share of the world's trade in manufactures took place between the industrialized countries, there was greater dependence on the markets of Western Europe and the United States, and less on more slowly growing markets in the primary producing areas. Technological progress generated new currents of trade as industrialized countries built up comparative advantages through national and regional specialization. In fact movements of factors between industrialized countries and the gradual spread of technical knowledge ironed out many of national and regional differences, but the Heckscher-Olin Theory, that international trade depends on these differences, might be disputed at this time as trade between the industrialized countries producing similar commodities steadily increased. The range of commodities which could be produced for export was widened, and a growing proportion of the Gross National Product (in Britain it was about a quarter in 1951) was exported.

The growth of the Gross National Product was therefore a most important factor in the export performance, even though increases in trade occurred at a higher rate than economic growth. World trade was growing at more than 9 per cent p.a. while manufacturing output increased at 5 per cent p.a. This trend continues through the decade and will be examined later.

International institutions

In the previous decade some attempts had been made to remove the restrictions on trade and payments and to set up international institutions to help trade to flow more freely. The I.M.F. was helping to overcome the chronic shortage of international payments media, especially of dollars, and the E.P.U. was easing the payments system within Europe. Some easing of quotas and trade discrimination was possible.

Technological progress

The growing effectiveness of this policy was another factor in the expansion of trade, and this in turn helped export industries to increase the scale of their production, bringing vast economies of scale. In chemicals, motor, aircraft, and other engineering and metallurgical industries where the optimum size of plant is very large, the growth of export markets made possible expanded lower-cost production, and the huge investment programmes essential to technological progress. While the 'advances in industrial technology often conferred on individual countries and on firms within them economic advantages capable of stimulating commercial exchanges across frontiers' (Postan). Thus the export industries were growth industries and the growth industries were export industries, and the fears that trade would diminish as the economics of the leading industrial nations became more alike were soon dispelled. Technical advances gave countries essentially temporary comparative advantages such as Britain enjoyed in nuclear power and in jet aircraft in the early 1950s.

Business confidence

The rise in the level of business confidence was partly responsible for the growth of exports 1946–51. In the inter-war years the commercial and financial transactions associated with international trade had helped to spread depressions round the world. In the post-war period international trade was an important factor in the economics of industrialized economies and provided buoyancy when other sectors were depressed. As the fears and uncertainties associated with international payments were removed and the boom in world trade continued, businessmen gained in confidence, and investment in the export industries supported the flow of factors into this sector and fostered the growth rate. It was the demand for capital equipment both to replace that damaged or worn out during the war and to facilitate the growth of industries as well as the upsurge in consumer demand in North America, Western Europe and Australasia, and the growing facilities for international trade, that was at the heart of the world boom, and the eager market for Britain's exports. 'Money, specialist agencies, export advice and goodwill were thus all active in providing world development and international trade after the war. Few countries stood to gain more than Britain, always provided that brains, thrift and enterprise could maintain her industrial efficiency' (Youngson).

The unfavourable growth rate of Britain's exports

The export performance was not without criticism. Several other industrialized countries had a significantly better record than Britain, and her share of World exports fell from more than 28 per cent to 24 per cent in the period 1948–51, and by the end of the decade 1948–58 her share was down to 21 per cent (cf. 22·4 per cent in 1937). Yet the value of Britain's exports increased in value from $6·3 billion in 1950 to $9·4 billion in 1958. At the same time, however, the U.S. exports grew from $10·3 billion to $18 billion, Germany from $2 billion to $8·8 billion and Japan from less than $1 billion to almost $3 billion. The French also had a better growth performance in the value of exports than Britain in the period 1950–58, with an increase of nearly 70 per cent to over $5 billion.

A marked correlation between the growth of industrial production in different countries over the decade and the growth in their exports of manufactures has been pointed out by Worswick and Ady. The figures they present in *The British Economy in the 1950s* show that the countries with the greatest growth in industrial production also enjoyed the greatest rise in manufactured exports.

	Growth of Industrial Production 1950–52 cf. 1957–59	*Rise in Manufactured Exports 1950–52 cf. 1957–59*
	%	%
Britain	23	17
U.S.A.	19	30
France	58	40
Germany	84	315
Japan	130	242

Britain's share in the export of the manufactures of the top eleven industrialized countries declined from nearly 30 per cent in 1948 to 18 per cent in 1958 while Germany increased her share from 8 per cent to 19 per cent. Even in the period 1954–58 Britain's share of the

Western European market declined from 16 per cent to 13 per cent and of the sterling area countries (not in O.E.C.D.) from 58 per cent to 51 per cent. Both Germany and Japan enjoyed a faster increase in the rate of industrial production and an increase in the proportion of industrial products exported.

INDUSTRIAL PRODUCTION

1958 = 100

	Britain	*E.E.C*	*U.S.A.*	*Industrial top 11*
1948	72	73	73	64
1958	100	100	100	100

The reasons for the unfavourable growth rate

A number of reasons have been advanced to explain Britain's export performance in the decade 1948–58, which was good when compared with preceding decades, but poor when compared with other leading industrial nations. Some of the main reasons offered are listed below:

1. A decline in the proportion of the Gross National Product going into exports.
2. Fully employed resources preventing export industries expanding to meet world demand.
3. The rise in money wages as related to productivity – and the relatively rapid increase in the prices of Britain's exports as compared with those of her main competitors.
4. Britain's commitment to the production and export of goods in which world demand was rising relatively slowly.
5. The greater dependence on markets in primary producing countries where demand was rising less fast.
6. The decline in protection for British goods in markets in the Commonwealth and Sterling Area.
7. The recurrent balance of payments crisis made necessary the use of physical controls and monetary and fiscal policies which were deflationary, and restricted growth.

N.B. The reader would find it profitable to investigate the factors affecting the growth rates of other countries.

In an earlier chapter we have seen that the proportion of the British National Income which derives from international trade is very large, though no larger than that of several other countries in Western Europe. Although the share of Britain's resources going into international trade has varied during the period covered in this study, these variations have not been highly significant. In the decade 1948–58 the proportion of the Gross National Product going into exports reached a peak of 27 per cent in 1951 and fell to 22 per cent in 1958. In the post-war years there had been a more rapid growth of exports than of the Gross National Product, but the boom in consumer demand in the 1950s, especially during the more inflationary periods, had caused producers who were finding competition in export markets more severe, to look to the softer conditions in the domestic market.

The argument that Britain's failure to compete effectively in world markets had been largely due to the inflationary pressure caused by having too small a margin of unused potential, i.e. resources not fully employed, has been advanced by Professor Paish. Unused potential is a more significant determinant of the level of inflationary pressure since fluctuations in unemployment are not more than one-fifth as large as those in the margin of potential, partly because the rise in the margin is nearly twice as large as the fall in employment, and partly because the fall in employment is some two and a half times as large as the rise in unemployment. The running down of the margin of unused potential associated with an over-rapid rise of output to meet booms in world or domestic markets brings about shortages of materials, delays in deliveries and waiting lists. These shortages tend to increase the imports of materials and encourage stock accumulation, which further stimulates imports. In all these ways inflationary pressure is built up and the competitive position of British producers both in home and in export markets is affected. In the years 1952 to 1957 the margin of unused potential varied between 3·9 per cent and 0·5 per cent and averaged 2·3 per cent and Paish has shown that the balance of payments on current account was in deficit only once during these six years, and that was in 1955 (— £155m) when the unused potential was only 0·5 per cent.

The rise in labour costs associated with periods when the margin of unused potential is low was excessive when compared with those of other leading industrial nations. The index of labour costs increased from 86 in 1952 to 115 in 1958.

Again, taking 1958 as the base year, it is striking that while the index of industrial production rises from 81 in 1948 to 100 in 1958, the index of wages and salaries rises from 52. Although the export prices of British manufactures increased by much less than labour costs, they increased faster than those of most of their industrial rivals. Taking 1958 as 100 the relative price index in 1953 was U.S.A. (89), Germany (100), Japan (108), France (98), Italy (116), while Britain was 91. In Germany labour costs were also rising, indeed there was a rise of 55 per cent in hourly earnings in the manufacturing industries if we compare the average of between 1953–55 with 1958–61, while in Britain the rise was only 43 per cent, but the much faster rise in the productivity of the German manufacturing industries ensured that the rise in unit labour costs would be much smaller (11 per cent) than that in Britain (22 per cent).

Declining markets

The argument that Britain depended more heavily than her rivals on trade with the primary producers, where demand was rising less rapidly than in the industrial nations, is difficult to sustain as a major factor in Britain's relatively poor export performance. Britain's dependence on these markets, and on the export of the products of industries which were suffering a decline, as in textiles, was greater than that of her rivals. We have seen that the progress of the industry up to 1951 when the exports were running at more than four times the 1938 level was encouraging. But by 1951 competition from Western Europe, Japan and India was becoming more and more effective, especially as costs of production in Britain were rising. (British cotton producers had to pay more for imported raw materials after devaluation.) The short but serious recession in 1951–52, associated with the opening of the Korean War, dealt a blow from which the industry never recovered. 'The industry's position in the scheme of international comparative advantages was fundamentally weak' (Pollard).

The woollen industry also suffered heavily, after an even more successful growth up to 1951. Concentration on high quality exports to North America provided a measure of recovery, but Italy gradually stepped up the competition to become the leading exporter of woollens. By mixing more and more artificial fibres with wool the industry was able to compete for a while with other countries' products and with the new fibres, but the total value of exports, having reached £470m in 1951 from £293m in 1948, fell rapidly to £251m in 1958. Shipbuilding, man-made fibres, paper and railway stock all suffered a setback in 1951–52 from which they had hardly recovered by 1958.

Growth markets

But we have seen that Britain was concentrating on the production of capital and consumer goods which embodied a good deal of technical skill and were in the van of technological progress and for which international conditions were favourable. There was no real setback for these industries – cars, chemicals, aircraft, machinery and steel – even during the recessions in world demand which had affected textiles. The index of total production of chemicals increased from 59 in 1948 to 100 in 1958 and the value of chemical exports increased from £103m to £264m. The most successful items in this section were petro-chemicals and the other products of oil refining. In this period exports of petrol, gas, oil, diesel oil, fuel oil and plastics soared. The category which accounted for a larger percentage of Britain's exports than ever before was machinery and transport equipment. This had expanded rapidly from the end of the war (£82m in 1945 to £572m in 1948), continued its remarkable growth, and by 1958 had reached £1,356m. Britain and Germany were fighting for the leading position in the export of cars. In 1948 about 500 million cars and commercial vehicles were produced, (cf. 510 million pre-war peak) and a third of them were exported. By 1959 the total vehicle production was more than three times the 1948 level, of which exports were nearly one-half of the total. France, U.S. and Italy were intensifying competition in world export markets throughout this period. By 1958 Britain's chief exporters were machinery (17 per cent), vehicles and aircraft (12 per cent), chemicals (8 per cent) and electrical equipment (7 per cent). Compare this with 1938 when the leading categories were machinery (11 per cent), cotton (10 per cent) and coal (9 per cent).

Even with this new concentration on growth fields Britain's performance was not as good as that of other leading industrial nations – Japan, Germany, Italy, France and Sweden, and as a growing proportion of her trade was with industrial countries the effect on the balance of trade was inevitably adverse. Britain's trade with Western Europe – by 1958 two and a quarter times the 1948 level (£868m) – and with North America – three and a half times the 1948 level (£490m) – was rising more rapidly than trade with the rest of the Sterling Area (£1,404m in 1958) and with the rest of the world (£487m), both failing to double the 1948 value. This suggests that Britain's dependence on markets which were not in the leading industrial countries was declining although the Sterling Area still took one-third of the total value of her exports. The decline in the discrimination in favour of British goods in the markets of the Commonwealth and Sterling Area had not had much effect on the pattern of Britain's trade by 1958.

Effects of contra-cylical policies

The thesis that the contra-cyclical policies adopted by British Governments ('Stop-Go') to deal with balance of payments crisis adversely affected the growth of production and exports has many advocates. In the decade 1948–58 Britain was involved in financial crisis in 1949, 1951, 1956 and 1957. We have seen how the 1949 crisis led to devaluation in September of that year. With the outbreak of the Korean War, American stockpiling forced prices up and purchases in the Sterling Area brought a boom in trade. But the British Government was involved in a costly defence programme, involving invisible expenditure of £150m, while the rise in the prices of imports by more than 40 per cent in 1951–52 produced a greater trade deficit. With a £365m deficit on the current balance of payments, and such meagre reserves, confidence in sterling was falling away. To meet this the Government returned to monetary and fiscal policies, including a rise in Bank Rate (from 2–4 per cent) for the first time since the beginning of the war. The cheap money policy of keeping the Bank Rate low to encourage investment was over and through a succession of crises the Bank Rate rose to 7 per cent in 1958. It is difficult to assess the extent to which this impeded investment. The introduction of further import restrictions and a reduction in the rearmament programme, reducing Government expenditure overseas to £61m helped to bring a favourable balance of payments on current account in 1951, and it was not until 1955, when earnings from invisible exports failed to maintain their remarkable recovery of the 1950s, that the balance of payments was again in deficit (— £155m). It was this which frustrated the Government's aspirations to make the pound fully convertible. The Suez crisis of November 1956 encouraged the flight from the pound. Confidence in Britain's ability to balance its payments drained away as the blocking of the Canal involved Britain in extra costs and expenditure on oil from dollar sources. The fall in confidence was responsible for the erosion of the gold and dollar reserves and it was the persistent withdrawals and not a deficit in the balance of payments which brought about the 1957 crisis. The persistent inflation which produced a rise in the index of retail prices from 89 in 1955 to 97 in 1957 (1958 = 100) and uncertainty about exchange rates associated with rumours of revaluation of the mark and fear of revaluation of the pound intensified pressure on sterling. Further monetary measures, including the rise in the Bank Rate to 7 per cent brought about some improvement in 1958. The cyclical occurrences of crises in Britain's international financial situation initiated Government measures which undoubtedly inhibited the growth of Britain's trade. The 'Stop-Go' policies produced uncertainties which were frustrating the enterprises looking for opportunities of expanding production for the export market, and along with some of the reasons discussed above help to explain why Britain's share in exports had declined in almost every area except North America by 1958.

SUMMARY

1. There has been a considerable growth in Britain's imports (1968 = 7 times 1938 value) and exports (1968 = 10 times 1938) since the outbreak of the Second World War.

2. Britain's essential supplies in war-time were financed largely by borrowing (£3,000m) and the sale of overseas assets (£1,000m). The volume of imports was cut drastically because of difficulties in transport. Export markets were taken over by competitors less involved in the war, and export industries were adapted to war needs.

3. The output of home produced goods was expanded to reduce the need for imports. This 'import substitution' was particularly important in foodstuffs, and manufactured goods, but the need for basic materials increased.

4. The authorities responsible for international finance were determined that there would be no breakdown in confidence and co-operation after the War as had occurred after the First World War. The Bretton Woods Conference proposed the formation of the International Monetary Fund to act as a multilateral payments system, and the International Bank for Reconstruction and Development.

5. But the main problem was the critical shortage of dollars, and Lend-Lease, and Marshall Aid were more effective than the I.M.F. in alleviating this problem.

6. The General Agreement on Tariffs and Trade established in 1947 made some slow progress in a programme for the reduction of trade barriers. Britain's part in all these international institutions was limited by the imbalance in her own balance of payments.

7. A number of factors contributed to a situation in which the

devaluation of the pound from £1 = $4 to £1 = $2.80 seemed highly desirable:

(*a*) The limited success of the dollar-export drive.
(*b*) The attempt at making the pound fully convertible.
(*c*) The conversion of sterling balances into dollars.
(*d*) The continued growth of dollar imports.
(*e*) The decline in gold and convertible currency reserves.
(*f*) Persistent balance of payments deficits.

8. In the decade 1948–58 Britain's exports increased at a faster rate than in any decade since the First World War. Exporters were concentrating more on growth sectors in world trade, and a greater proportion of the G.N.P. was exported.

9. Despite this the growth rate of Britain's exports did not compare favourably with those of Britain's rivals (see pp. 53–58).

10. The contra-cyclical ('Stop–Go') policies adopted by the Government to deal with recurrent balance of payments crises have been criticized for their unfavourable effects on export growth; but the insufficient margin of unused productive potential with the resultant inflationary pressures, was probably more important.

CHAPTER 5

BRITAIN'S TRADE IN THE LAST DECADE

1958-68

In the previous decade 1948 had, conveniently, marked the beginning of certain trends. 1958 cannot in the same way be regarded as a turning point, although it was in some ways an exceptional year. Once before 1956 in the pre-war period, the visible part of the Balance of Payments on Current Account (the Balance of Trade) had been favourable. In 1958 not only was there a surplus of exports and re-exports (£3,407m) over imports (£3,378m) of £29m, but with the greatest earnings on invisible items (£526m) ever achieved before 1962, the balance on the current account was more favourable (£336m) than at any time in Britain's history. The years 1956 to 1959 were remarkable in that Britain earned some £900m in favourable balances on current account, and Britain's gold and convertible currency reserves, along with unused I.M.F. drawing rights (taken together) continued to grow until 1960:

	Gold and convertible currency	*£m I.M.F. drawing rights*
1956	799	347
1957	812	345
1958	1,096	351
1959	977	720
1960	1,154	871

However it should be noted that these reserves were small when compared with Britain's liabilities in the form of sterling balances (over £4,000m).

Just as in the previous decade, the swings of the trade cycle had brought three crises associated with adverse balance of payments, and a decline in confidence and flight from sterling, so in the decade 1958–68 there have been three cycles, with crises in 1960, 1964, and

1967. The pattern of expansion leading to a balance of payments crisis, followed by recession, has become chronic in the last decade, with crises more severe than ever before. The demands being made on the home economy, and the economies of her trading partners have been so excessive as to bring Britain's balance of payments into fundamental disequilibrium. Only heavy borrowing has enabled Britain to maintain her already all-too-meagre reserves of gold and convertible currencies:

	Gold and convertible currency	*I.M.F.*		*Gold and convertible currency*	*I.M.F*
1961:	£1,185	497	1965:	£1,073	16
1962:	£1,002	876	1966:	£1,107	205
1963:	£949	871	1967:	£1,123*	594
1964:	£827	512	1968:	see p.80	

* at new parity £1 = £2.40, 18th Nov.

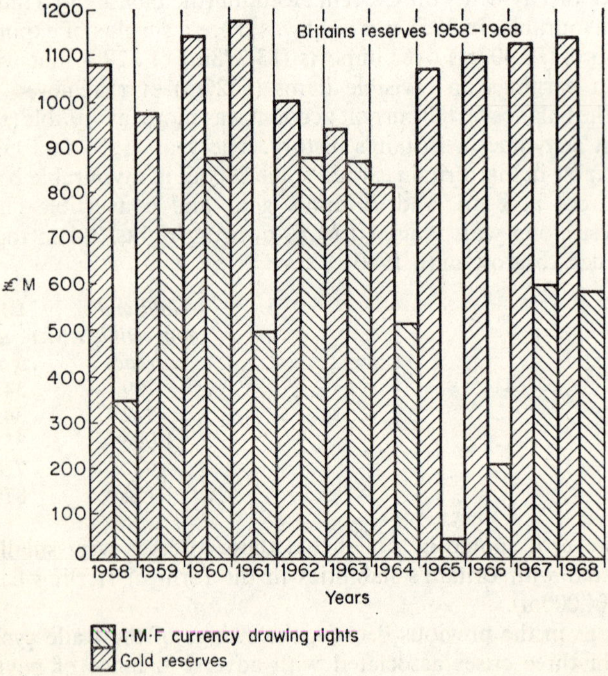

A recent D.E.A. progress report pointed out that 'International help for sterling in the recent foreign exchange crisis has bolstered the total in the last three years. Such help is usually provided by other countries buying sterling from the U.K. authorities in exchange for their own currency. The currency is added to the U.K.'s reserves; the sterling adds to those countries' sterling holding.' Thus the steady increase in Britain's liabilities to other countries and international organizations is illustrated partly by the rise in the sterling balances:

1962 = £3,737m	1964 = £4,273m	1966 = £5,145m
1963 = £3,861m	1965 = £4,844m	1967 = see p.80

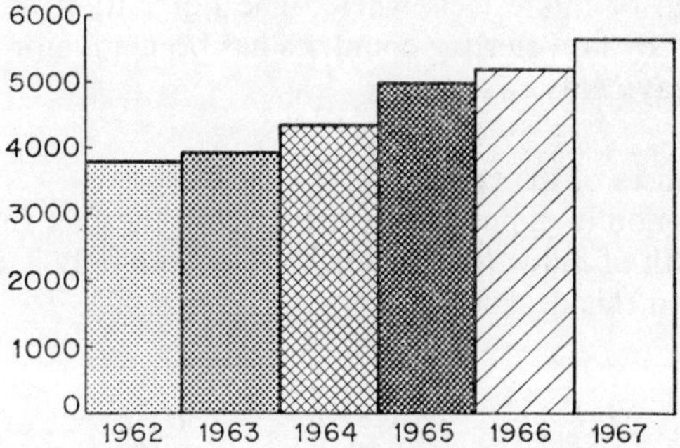

Sterling Balances

The Sterling Balances are not an adequate indicator of Britain's indebtedness however, because they do not include all the considerable short-term borrowing from international institutions and other Central Bankers intended to support sterling during the crisis periods. Three main categories make up the balances. Firstly, the working balances held by monetary authorities or central banks of a number of overseas countries in order to supply their own traders with the sterling with which to obtain goods from the Sterling Area. Secondly, the reserve holdings of foreign banks and individuals, which are kept in London for security. Thirdly, funds placed in this country to take advantage of the numerous opportunities of profitable investment. Apart from the liabilities to international institutions, about 60 per cent of the balances are held by other Central Banks and official monetary institutions; much of the remainder being in the hands of foreign commercial banks and traders. They are held in a variety of ways: in deposit with banks (approximately 40 per cent), in Treasury Bills (29 per cent), in British Government Stocks (approximately 27 per cent), and in local authorities and finance companies (4 per cent).

The balances all represent loans of money and resources to Britain but there are some claims (about £1,225m in 1966) by Britain on other countries to set against this. That the balances are a source of instability has been illustrated in the balance of payments crises of the last decade. When people abroad doubt our ability to repay the balances on demand or to maintain their value, there is a tendency to use them to buy foreign currencies or gold from our reserves. The reserves are also reduced by the withdrawal of funds attracted by a higher rate of interest elsewhere. The liquidation of the sterling reserves held by non-sterling countries has been a major factor in the balance of payments crisis.

The main causes of the crises

Britain's economic difficulties centre around the fact that while her rate of growth of industrial production has been only half that of her main rivals in this decade

	Britain	*E.E.C. Countries*	*U.S.A.*	*Industrial Top 11*
1958 =	100	100	100	100
1966 =	135	163	167	168

any attempt to accelerate the rate of growth leads to a balance of payments crisis: e.g. the expansionist policy associated with the Plan of the National Economic Development Council established in 1962, and supported by the 'expansion without inflation' budget of 1963, was followed by a deficit of £402m on the current account of the balance of payments in 1964. Exports had increased by a mere 2 per cent 1961–63 (cf. N.E.D.C. expected 5 per cent) while imports had risen by 6 per cent.

Some writers regard these crises in the balance of payments as being the main cause of Britain's relatively poor growth performance. Britain comes low in the league table for the average annual increase in output – (the G.N.P. at constant market prices) for the period 1958–64.

GROWTH PERFORMANCE

Country	*Average ann. incr. in output* %	*per head* %
Japan	10·4	8·8
W. Germany	6·3	5·0
Italy	5·7	5·6
Sweden	5·4	3·9
France	5·2	4·9
Denmark	5·0	3·8
Belgium	3·6	3·0
Britain	3·1	2·6
U.S.	3·1	2·0

But Professor Paish considers that the markedly adverse balance of payments following on an over rapid increase in output is largely due to a fall in the margin of unused productive potential. The produc-

1958 = 100

	Britain G.N.P.	*Indices of indus. prod.*	*Imports*	*Exports*	*Unemployed ,000*	*Unfilled vacancies ,000*
1962	114	115	121	120	422	149
1963	118	119	130	130	500	144
1964	125	128	148	136	361	221
1965	129	132	150	145	309	265
1966	131	133	158	155	325	255
1967	132	133	168	155	515	174
April 1968		137	204	179	511	186

Year	*Average potential in use* %	*Stock accumulation* £m	*Visible balance of trade* £m	*Balance of payments on current account* £m
1958	94	111	+ 29	+ 347
1959	95·6	174	− 118	+ 149
1960	*98·2*	*602*	*− 408*	*− 258*
1961	97·2	334	− 153	+ 5
1962	95·3	83	− 104	+ 127
1963	95·8	228	− 83	+ 116
1964	*97·9*	*649*	*− 545*	*− 402*
1965	97·8	416	− 281	− 110
1966	97·0	209	− 152	− 59

Figures from L.B.R. April 1968

tive potential of the country is the physical limit on output, and it depends on existing resources, institutions, attitudes and tastes. Shortages of fixed capital, of raw materials, of semi-finished goods, or of transport facilities can impose a limit even before the reserve of unemployed labour is used up, but this has been the main limiting factor in Britain since the war. It can be seen on page 65 that the decline in the number of unemployed and the rise in the numbers of unfilled vacancies coincides with a slowing down in the rate of growth of Britain's industrial production from 1963 to 1966. The margin of unused potential is defined as the difference between the gross domestic product (the growth of output) and the productive potential. There are three main effects (on the balance of payments) of the running down of the margin of productive potential. Firstly, the rapid rise in output leads to a sharp increase in stock accumulation and in imports. Secondly, as the margin shrinks it becomes increasingly difficult to meet deadlines; and soon there are shortages, lengthening order books and delays in delivery. Thirdly, and more seriously, the over expansion is accompanied by 'a permanent and largely irreversible rise of costs and prices'.

MANUFACTURED EXPORT PRICES

	British labour costs per unit of output	*Britain*	*U.S.*	*France*	*Germany*	*Italy*	*Japan*
1959 =	100	100	100	100	100	100	100
1966 =	128	117	115	112	106	101	90

Paish suggests that 'with the rise of British costs, the rise of export prices of British manufactures has been too little for them to be profitable . . . (but) too much for them to be competitive'.

Others have argued that the 'panic measures' taken by the Government have exaggerated the crises. In 1964 the 15 per cent surcharge on imports (excepting food and raw materials) aroused the hostility of our trading partners (contravened the G.A.T.T.), especially as no restraints were placed on domestic demand, and higher social benefits were announced. Withdrawal of funds from London assumed alarming proportions, and some $3,000m emergency credit facilities made available by other Central Banks were necessary to restore confidence in the Pound. In the 1966–67 crisis it required a devaluation and even more massive credit facilities to halt the flight from the £.

Britain's invisible earnings

We have seen that before the First World War the surplus on invisible items was more than sufficient to meet the deficit on visible items. Undoubtedly this surplus was a powerful factor in building up confidence in the pound. The table on p.68 illustrates that surpluses on invisible items have been getting smaller, and in recent years have been unable to cover the heavy deficit on visible items. This has been another factor in the crisis of confidence in the pound.

There are three basic reasons why the surplus on invisible items has failed to grow enough to meet the deficit on visible items.

(*a*) The amount paid for invisible items obtained abroad has increased steadily in the last decade. These payments have been for tourism, interest on loans from foreigners, and transport services.

(*b*) Although there has been an increase in the value of invisible items sold to foreigners, these have only just kept pace with our increased payments for invisible items. The predominance of the City of London in financial services is less certain, while the flow of funds for investment abroad has been declining recently.

(*c*) The huge increase in Government expenditure (especially military expenditure) abroad is a highly important factor in declining surplus on invisible items (see page 70).

The composition of Britain's invisible earnings

Table of items, 1966

	Item	*Import £m*	*Export £m*
1.	Government	504	43
2a.	Shipping	752	767
b.	Civil aviation	153	177
3.	Travel	297	219
4.	Other services	355	624
5.	Interest, profits and dividends	568	967
6.	Private transfers	180	128

1. *Government payments and receipts*. It can be seen from the above table that the remarkable increase in the payments abroad made by the Government to meet the cost of the armed forces and the services provided by Consuls and Embassies, has been stemmed in 1967. Government receipts go but a small way towards meeting

BRITAIN'S BALANCE OF PAYMENTS 1946–67

£m	*Av. 1946–51*	*Av. 1952–54*	*Av. 1955–57*	*1958*	*1959*	*1960*	*1961*	*1962*	*1963*	*1964*	*1965*	*1966*	*1967*
Imports	2,022	2,988	3,416	3,378	3,640	4,141	4,045	4,098	4,370	5,016	5,065	5,263	5,673
Exports and re-exports	1,773	2,746	3,320	3,407	3,522	3,733	3,892	3,994	4,287	4,471	4,784	5,116	5,023
Visible balance	−249	−242	−96	+29	−118	−408	−153	−104	−83	−545	−281	−147	−630
Invisible balance	141	384	189	307	254	133	148	205	190	150	163	116	136
Current balance	−108	+142	+92	+336	+136	−275	−5	+101	+107	−395	−118	−31	−51

Taken from the Report of the Committee on Invisible Exports

BRITAIN'S BALANCE OF PAYMENTS 1968
IN £ MILLION. SEASONALLY ADJUSTED

Current account	*1967*	*1968 1st quarter*	*1968 2nd quarter*
Imports (f.o.b.)	5660	1692	1692
Exports and re-exports	5023	1477	1442
Visible trade balance	−637	−215	−250
Government transactions	−453	−116	−111
Other invisible items	+686	+163	+192
Current balance	−404	−168	−169
Capital account			
Official transactions	−57	−37	+17
Private investment abroad	424	180	159
Foreign investment in U.K.	395	85	117
Balance of long-term capital	−86	−132	−25
Balance of current and capital accounts	−490	−300	−194
Balance of monetary movements	315	331	100

From Bank of England Quarterly Bulletin.

these payments and have fallen from a peak of £46m in 1965 to £36m in 1967. The stringent measures of 1967 designed to produce economies in Government expenditure achieved a measure of success. However this has been partly at the expense of *Government economic aid* which after rising from £161m in 1962, to £208m in 1966, was cut back to £198m in 1967.

2. *Transport.* The great days in which Britain's shipping added over £100m to the surpluses of invisible items have gone. The receipts accruing from the use of Britain's ships has continued to grow:

1962	*1963*	*1964*	*1965*	*1966*	*1967*
647	662	703	752	767	877

but the payments made by Britain to other's shipping to carry her goods has also increased:

1962	*1963*	*1964*	*1965*	*1966*	*1967*
668	688	739	750	752	808

BRITAIN'S INVISIBLE ITEMS 1946–67

£m	*Av. 1946–51*	*Av. 1952–54*	*Av. 1955–57*	*1958*	*1959*	*1960*	*1961*	*1962*	*1963*	*1964*	*1965*	*1966*	*1967*	*1968*
Payments				1,510	1,569	1,738	1,744	1,765	1,862	2,042	2,197	2,305	2,426	
Receipts				2,036	2,050	2,145	2,225	2,331	2,435	2,625	2,806	2,882	3,011	
Surplus	307	470	341	526	481	416	481	566	573	585	609	577	585	
Net Government expenditure	166	86	152	219	227	283	333	361	383	433	446	461	449	

so that for the years 1962–64 shipping was a debit item on the invisible balance. There has been a significant improvement in the last three years so that in 1967 shipping made a contribution of £69m to the invisible earnings. The contribution of civil aviation has remained steady around £23m p.a. 1962–67.

3. *Travel.* The measures introduced by the government in 1966 to restrict the amount spent by tourists abroad has played some part in halting the steady rise in this form of expenditure from £210m in 1962 to £297m in 1966. In 1967 it was £284m, and as the amount spent by foreign tourists in Britain continued to increase, 1962 £183m, 1966 £219m, 1967 £245m, the deficit on this item was reduced from £97m in 1965 to £39m in 1967.

4. *Interest profits and dividends.* The serious decline in the contribution of these items to the favourable invisible balance is due to the steep decline in earnings while payments had continued to grow:

	1962	*1963*	*1964*	*1965*	*1966*	*1967*
Earnings	766	845	899	1002	967	896
Payments	420	443	490	555	568	600

So that in 1967 the surplus was the lowest for many years:

	1962	*1963*	*1964*	*1965*	*1966*	*1967*
Surplus	346	402	409	447	399	296

5. *Other services.* It is fortunate that a considerable rise in the earnings from these items (from £525m in 1962 to £765m in 1967) was not balanced by as great a rise in Britain's payments for services (£254m to £373m) so that the increased surplus here (from £271m to £302m) offset the decrease in the previous group.

6. The surplus on invisible items has been eroded partly by the increase in *private transfer of funds* from Britain which has exceeded transfer to Britain by an increasing amount, each year since 1962, until in 1967 the deficit was £66m.

The fundamental weakness

It has long been recognized that the British economy is geared to a structural pattern in the balance of trade in which imports exceed exports. The trade deficits in recent years are therefore not new phenomena. But the recent balance of payments crises stem partly from a new weakness – the declining contribution of the invisible surplus. Although the heavy government expenditure has been a powerful contributor to this position, a reduction in government expenditure would merely have delayed the problems. The fundamental weakness has been the fact that the private invisible surplus has not grown fast enough in relation to the growth in the deficit on visible trade.

Short term effects of devaluation

On November 18, 1967 the £ sterling was devalued from £1 = $2.80 to £1 = $2.40, following weeks of intensive pressure on the pound through speculative monetary movements. Whatever the more lasting effects, there has been no increase in confidence in world currencies. The French franc has suffered similar pressure to that of sterling in 1968. The ability of the dollar to meet massive runs on the U.S. gold supply was severely tested early in 1968. But this chaos in international monetary circles has had the beneficial effect of bringing about growing co-operation among international financial powers in defence of each other's currencies, although Germany persists in an undervalued currency.

The immediate effect of devaluation was to reduce the price of Britain's exports in relation to the price of other countries' goods, while Britain's imports became more expensive in relation to home produced goods. The eventual effects of these changed price ratios (terms of trade) depends upon the elasticity of demand for Britain's exports and imports.

In the second and third quarters of 1968 there was evidence of the expected improvement in volume and value of exports. In sterling value terms exports and re-exports ran 25 per cent above the level of the corresponding quarters in 1967. The rise in the volume of exports was around 15 per cent—a lower level because of the rise in prices of exports to sterling area countries. The volume of world trade increased about 10 per cent in the same period. Some effort has been made to calculate what growth of exports would have been achieved without devaluation (*The Times*, November 18, 1968) and estimates vary between 8½ per cent and 10 per cent in dollar value.

There is obviously a time-lag during which the increased competitiveness of Britain's export prices begins to bite. By the end of the first half of 1968, exports had already made up what had been lost in lower prices. During 1969, the longer export orders will begin to affect the visible trade.

Export industries have enjoyed differing fortunes from devaluation. Those with inelastic markets have little to gain from lower export prices, and they have mostly taken the opportunity to raise their prices, thus increasing their revenue in sterling with no gain to Britain. The motor industry was expected to be among the leading beneficiaries for its markets are said to be highly competitive and elastic in demand. Although the industry had the spare capacity to meet an increase in demand, the series of labour problems throughout the first three-quarters of 1968 made it more difficult for the industry to take advantage of the situation. Despite this, more than ½ million vehicles had been exported in that period representing a 25 per cent increase in volume over the corresponding period in 1967. With the reduction in prices (around 7 per cent) and the increased cost of imported materials used in car manufacture, the improvement in the profitability of exporting by the industry was a good deal less than 25 per cent. Moreover the advantages enjoyed by the industry are gradually being eroded by inflation, and are likely to disappear by the end of 1969.

The biggest increase in the value of exports following devaluation has occurred in the chemical industry, where a growth of over 20 per cent has so far been recorded. But much of this benefit to the balance of payments has been eroded by an even greater growth of chemical imports (27 per cent). The heavy capital goods industries – shipbuilding, iron and steel, commercial vehicles, engineering (mechanical and electrical) products – have all expanded their exports and lengthened their order books. But again the effectiveness of their increases has been diminished by an increase in similar imports and by the increased cost of their imported materials. The industries where imported materials make up a large part of final costs have been hardest hit by devaluation. The increased cost of imported petroleum, iron ore, timber, tobacco, textile materials, and so on, have all affected prices of finished products in this country. This inflation soon erodes the increased price competitiveness gained by devaluation.

The need for further deflationary measures in November 1968, added to those which accompanied devaluation, and the April budget, have caused people to doubt whether the policy is proving effective. The biggest disappointment has been the behaviour of imports. In terms of foreign exchange the amount spent on imports has risen by 8 per cent. Consumer durables have been the worst offenders. Imports of refrigerators and washing machines have almost doubled, and there has been an increase of almost 30 per cent in the group. It is in an attempt to control spending in this sector that the government has introduced further restrictions on hire purchase and importers.

The total visible trade gap for 1968 will be close to £700m, bigger than for any year since 1951 when it was £749m. The huge rise in imports was mainly responsible for this deficit. In the first three quarters of 1967 imports valued £1,378m, £1,391m, £1,345m. In the first three quarters of 1968 the figures were £1,671m, £1,666m, £1,719 m. It is estimated that in the fourth quarter of 1968 Britain will pay out £1,740m, compared with £1,448m in the last quarter of 1967 (figures taken from *London & Cambridge Economic Bulletin*). The increase in the amount paid out for visible imports during the 1960's has been much greater than the growth of national earnings to pay for these imports. So a greater proportion of the national income is going to pay for imports. The failure of exporters to sell more abroad, and the failure of production to grow faster at home are fundamental reasons, but other factors have contributed to the faster growth of imports. The reduction of tariff barriers on all but agriculture goods as a result of agreements with E.F.T.A., with the Commonwealth, and through the Kennedy Round negotiations under G.A.T.T. The comparative cost advantages of Britain's products has been affected by the spread of technology and the growing efficiency of industries in Europe, Japan, and elsewhere. This has restricted our exporters in taking advantage of the same tariff reductions. In fact Britain's exports are running at over 20 per cent higher sterling values in 1968 than in the previous year, and more than 7 per cent in real terms.

The fastest rising category of imports in 1968 (16 per cent) has been manufactures, and it was in just this field that devaluation and restrictive measures was expected to bring reductions. In November the Chancellor announced the Customs and Excise regulator to increase rates on tobacco, oil, beer, wine, spirits and all rates of purchase tax; lower ceilings for bank lending in the private sector; and an import deposit of 50 per cent of the value of all imported goods other than basic foods, fuel and raw materials. With these measures the Government hopes to contain the growing propensity for imports which is at the heart of the growing balance of trade deficit.

Perhaps the only short-term conclusion to be made on the effectiveness of devaluation is that without it the increase in the value of exports would have been lower, and the increase in value of imports higher. The monthly trade deficits of 1968 would have been even greater. The reduction in the level of unemployment and the rise in money incomes would not have been so great, but the rise in the general level of prices would also have been less. Devaluation has provided no easy answer, but a breathing space within which the fundamental weaknesses in the balance of payments situation must be eradicated.

Some improvement in the performance of invisible items has been experienced in 1967 and 1968. For in 1967 the biggest surplus was achieved than in any year since 1959. The surplus of invisible items was £233m. The provisional estimates suggest that this surplus may exceed £250m in 1968. It appears that the beneficial effects of devaluation are showing first in the sphere of invisible trade.

A recent article (*Bank of England Quarterly Bulletin*, December 1968) has outlined the growing value of *direct net earnings from abroad of financial and similar institutions*, which has averaged £235m a year 1965–67. They are made up of:

Banking	£25m
Insurance	£110m
Merchanting ..	£35m
Other	£65m
	£235m

These are estimates and no attempt has been made to assess the indirect earnings of these institutions. The earnings from private services including the City of London's financial services, were up by £40m in 1967 on the average of the three previous years.

That part of the government's spending abroad which is paid in sterling, e.g. the sterling aid, is unaffected by devaluation, but it is estimated that some £10m has been added to that part of the bill paid in foreign exchange. Although the military spending east of Suez has been reduced, the foreign exchange cost of the forces in Germany has been increased by devaluation. The cut in commitments has enabled the Government to keep the spending in 1968 at about the same level as in 1967.

The effect of the restrictions on the amount that tourists from Britain can spend in foreign currencies was already evident in 1967, when total spending on travel and tourism was below the 1966 level. In 1968 the gap between the amount Britons spend abroad in this way, and the amount foreigners spend here, is expected to be closed even further.

The amount of interest Britain has to pay on her non-sterling debts abroad has been increased as devaluation has increased the sterling value of these debts. But the net effect of this is almost cancelled out by the corresponding increase in the sterling value of our investments abroad. The total net earnings of interest, profits and dividends have remained around £400m since 1966. Shipping and civil aviation continue to make a small contribution to the surplus on invisible items.

APPENDIX: STATISTICS OF OVERSEAS TRADE

IMPORTS AND EXPORTS BY AREAS

Monthly Average £m

Area	*Total Value of Imports (c.i.f.)*			*Total Value of Exports (f.o.b.)*		
	1965	*1966*	*1967*	*1965*	*1966*	*1967*
Sterling Area	150·02	147·93	147·10	136·61	132·13	127·22
Canada	*38·19*	*35·41*	*38·04*	*16·72*	*17·95*	*17·79*
U.S.A.	*36·02*	*60·24*	*67·66*	*41·63*	*52·16*	*51·12*
North America	94·21	95·66	105·70	58·34	70·10	68·92
E.F.T.A.	*65·20*	*69·98*	*78·46*	*55·57*	*61·64*	*63·19*
E.E.C.	*82·89*	*91·96*	*105·42*	*75·40*	*79·75*	*80·30*
Total Western Europe	157·93	172·26	195·17	144·72	157·98	159·21
Eastern Europe	18·34	20·06	21·16	9·45	12·23	13·96
Latin America	23·58	23·53	24·39	13·22	13·32	13·90
Rest of World	35·18	36·13	43·27	31·65	34·83	35·62
Total Non-Sterling	329·24	347·63	389·69	257·38	288·45	291·60
Total All Countries	479·26	495·57	536·80	394·00	420·58	418·82

VALUE OF COMMODITIES IN U.K. EXPORTS

The Value of Commodities in U.K. Exports. (A) (B) £ thousand
For month of January, 1968

0. *Food and Live Animals:*	Total:	13,694
01. Live animals		841
02. Dairy products and eggs		1,015
03. Fish and fish preparations		957
04. Cereals and cereal preparations		4,201
05. Fruit and vegetables		1,543
06. Sugar, sugar preparations and honey		1,897
07. Coffee, cocoa and preparations, tea and spices		1,216
Other food and food preparations		2,024
1. *Beverages and Tobacco:*	Total:	19,085
11. Beverages		16,751
12. Tobacco		2,334
2. *Crude Materials, Inedible:*	Total:	12,247
23. Crude rubber (inc. synthetic and reclaimed)		1,222
26. Textile fibres (not manufactured and their waste)		5,832
27. Crude fertilizers and minerals		2,205
Other crude materials		2,988
3. *Mineral Fuels, Lubricants, etc.:*	Total:	15,799
33. Petroleum and petroleum products		14,502
Coal, coke, gas and electrical energy		1,298
4. *Animal and Vegetable Oils and Fats:*	Total:	540
5. *Chemicals:*	Total:	43,970
51. Chemical elements and compounds		10,926
53. Dyeing, tanning and colouring materials		3,179
54. Medicinal and pharmaceutical products		7,507
55. Essential oils and perfume materials		3,735
57. Explosives and pyrotechnic products		774
58. Plastic materials and artificial resins		8,124
All other		7,724
6. *Manufactured goods classed chiefly by material:*	Total:	117,466
61. Leather, leather manufactures and dressed furs		2,768
62. Rubber manufactures, n.e.s.		4,683
64. Paper, paperboard and manufactures thereof		5,002
65. Textile, yarn, fabrics and articles		22,096

66. Non-metallic mineral manufactures (B)	28,356
67. Iron and steel	18,972
68. Non-ferrous metals	21,983
Other wood and metal manufactures	13,605
7. *Machinery and Transport Equipment:*	Total: 211,866
71. Machinery other than electric	103,542
72. Electrical machinery, apparatus and appliances	33,911
73. Transport equipment	74,413
8. *Miscellaneous Manufactured Articles:*	Total: 36,365
81. Sanitary, plumbing, heating, lighting, fittings	1,047
82. Furniture	1,335
84. Clothing	3,706
85. Footwear	1,669
86. Professional, scientific and controlling instruments; photographic and optical goods: watches and clocks	10,989
Other	17,619
5–8. *Manufactured Goods:*	Total: 409,667
9. *Commodities and Transactions not classified according to kind (A)*	Total: 11,249
TOTAL UNITED KINGDOM EXPORTS	482,283

VALUE OF BRITAIN'S IMPORTS AND EXPORTS
MONTHLY AVERAGE £M

Year	*Quarters*	*Imports*	*Exports and re-exports*
1967	1	536	445
	2	540	446
	3	508	395
	4	563	389
1968	1	647	496
	2	642	489
	3	667	530

VALUE AND VOLUME OF THE EXTERNAL TRADE OF U.K.

	IMPORTS						*EXPORTS*					
					Manufactured goods				*Manufactured goods*			
Year	*Total*	*Food Beverage Tobacco*	*Basic materials*	*Fuels*	*Semi Finished*	*Finished*	*Total*	*Chemicals*	*Classified chiefly by material*	*Machinery transport equipment*	*Other*	*Re-exports*
1957	344·9	123·2	97·1	38·8	62·0	22·3	281·2	22·4	83·8	109·2	15·9	10·8
1958	319·5	124·1	75·5	36·6	56·2	25·3	270·8	22·0	75·5	113·0	15·7	11·8
1959	340·6	126·6	78·8	38·9	62·5	31·4	285·2	24·6	78·9	119·7	16·4	10·9
1960	387·9	128·3	90·0	40·0	83·8	43·1	304·0	26·6	82·4	127·7	18·2	11·8
1961	378·9	123·7	84·1	40·2	81·3	46·3	316·3	27·3	84·1	135·5	19·7	13·2
1962	385·6	130·8	77·1	44·4	79·6	50·1	325·4	28·6	84·4	138·4	21·1	13·1
1963	415·3	139·7	82·5	46·5	87·5	54·3	350·9	30·7	86·9	150·6	23·4	12·8
1964	474·7	147·6	93·2	48·6	110·3	69·7	367·6	34·3	94·8	152·5	26·3	12·8
1965	479·3	142·3	92·4	50·8	114·3	73·5	394·0	36·8	100·9	165·6	29·8	14·4
1966	495·6	142·6	88·4	52·1	123·3	82·6	420·6	39·1	104·1	181·7	31·6	16·2
1967	536·8	147·1	84·4	60·9	133·4	103·6	418·8	41·1	104·8	175·6	34·3	15·4

Monthly averages in £m

CHANGES IN STERLING RESERVES AND LIABILITIES

		Reserves: Gold and convertible currency	Liabilities			
			Total	*International organization*	*£ area*	*Non £ area*
1966		1107	5145	1656	2589	900
1967		1123	5346	1540	2443	1353
1968	1.	1134	5693	1543	2545	1595
	2.	1118	5633	2136	2172	1314
	3.	1132	5832			1469
	4.	1009				

1968 SEASONALLY ADJUSTED VALUES OF U.K. EXPORTS AND IMPORTS BY SELECTED AREAS (MONTHLY AVERAGE £M)

Quarters		*Total*	*Sterling area*	*Canada*	*U.S.A.*	*Western Europe*	*Latin America*	*Eastern Europe*	*Rest of World*
Exports 1968	1.	496	150	23	70	178	18	18	42
	2.	486	142	19	69	181	19	18	42
	3.	530	148	21	78	195	18	18	52
Imports 1968	1.	647	184	45	82	242	24	25	42
	2.	642	187	45	83	232	26	25	47
	3.	667	190	41	94	242	27	26	49

BIBLIOGRAPHY

Reports on Overseas Trade, Board of Trade, H.M.S.O. (monthly).
Board of Trade Journal, H.M.S.O. (weekly).
Annual Abstract of Statistics, H.M.S.O.
Monthly Digest of Statistics, H.M.S.O.
Economic Trends, H.M.S.O.
The British Economy: Key Statistics, London and Cambridge Economic Service (*The Times*).
Export Trends, National Economic Development Council, H.M.S.O.
A Study of U.K. Imports, M. F. Scott, Cambridge.
Britain's Invisible Earnings, Report of the Committee.
The British Economy in the 1950's, Worswick and Ady, Oxford.
The Development of the British Economy, S. Pollard, Arnold.
Britain's Economic Growth 1920–66, A. J. Youngson,
An Economic History of England, William Ashworth, Methuen.
Britain and the World Economy, Livingstone, Penguin.
The City in the World Economy, William M. Clarke, Penguin.
Problems of the World Economy, Richard Bailey, Penguin.
Guide to the British Economy, Peter Donaldson, Penguin.
An Economic History of Modern Britain, J. H. Clapham, Cambridge.
British Economic Policy since the War, Andrew Schonfield, Penguin.
The U.K. Economy, A. R. Prest, Weidenfeld and Nicolson.
Economic Survey 1919–39, W. A. Lewis,
The Economic History of Western Europe 1945–64, M. M. Postan,
A Concise Economic History of Britain 1750 to recent times, W. H. B. Court, Cambridge.
Britain in the World Economy, A. E. Kahn,
The Trade Cycle, R. C. O. Matthews,
Studies in an Inflationary Economy, F. W. Paish,
Studies in British Overseas Trade, 1870–1914, S. B. Saul, Liverpool Univ. Press.
British Export Performance, S. J. Wells, Cambridge.
International Economics, C. R. Kindleberger, Irwin.

International Monetary Co-operation 1945–65, B. Tew, Hutchinson.
British Overseas Trade from 1700 to the 1930's, W. Schlote (translated Henderson & Chaloner).
The Migration of British Capital to 1875, L. H. Jenks.
The British Economy of the 19th Century, W. W. Rostow.
Home and Foreign Investment 1870–1913, A. K. Cairncross.
The Management of the British Economy, 1945–60, J. C. R. Dow.
The British Economy in 1975, ed. W. Beckerman,
International Trade and Economic Growth, H. G. Johnson, Allen & Unwin.
British War Economy, Hancock & Gowing, H.M.S.O.
The Radcliffe Report, The Workings of the Monetary System.
Britain and the European Community 1955–1963, M. Camp, Princeton.

Articles

'Britain and World Trade 1870–1914', S. B. Saul, *E. H. R. 2nd Series VII.*
'Real Values in British Foreign Trade', A. H. Imlah, *J. E. H. 1948.*
'The Terms of Trade of the U.K. 1798–1913', A. H. Imlah, *J. E. H. 1950.*
'British Balance of Payments and Export of Capital', A. H. Imlah, *E.H.R. 2nd Series V – No. 2 1952.*
'The Management of the British Economy', F. W. Paish, *L.B.R. April 1965.*
'How the Economy Works', F. W. Paish, *L.B.R. April, 1965.*
'Re-thinking Foreign Trade Policy', E. A. G. Robinson, *Three Banks Review.*
'The Changing Structure of the British Economy', E. A. G. Robinson, *E.J. 1954.*
'E.F.T.A. – The End of the Transition', S. J. Wells, *L.B.R., October 1966.*
'How Fast can Britain Grow', A. Maddison, *L.B.R. January, 1966.*
'Britain's Growth Performance: The Enigma of the 1950's', Knapp & Lomax, *C.B.R., October 1964.*
'Capital Movements in the 20th Century', J. H. Dunning, *L.B.R. April, 1964.*
'Sterling: the Problem of Policy, A. R. Conan, *W.B.R. November 1967.*
'The International Finance Corporation', D. Grenier, *W.B.R. May 1966.*

'Reforming the International Monetary System', A. Day, *W.B.R. August 1964.*

'The Impact of Post War Capital Movements, A. R. Conan, *W.B.R. August 1963.*

'The Role of Invisible Trade in the U.K. balance of payments 1952–66', F. N. Burton and P. Galambos, *N.P.B.R. May 1968.*

'The Role of Overseas Investment in the U.K. Balance of Payments', A. F. B. Williams, *W.B.R. May, 1965.*

L.B.R. – Lloyds Bank Review.
N.P.B.R. – National Provincial Bank Review.
W.B.R. – Westminster Bank Review.
E.H.R. – Economic History Review.
J.E.H. – Journal of Economic History.
E.J. – Economic Journal.

ESSAY QUESTIONS

1. Outline the changes in the pattern of Britain's trade since the War (J.M.B.).
2. Describe the measures available to the Government to deal with an adverse balance of payments and discuss the circumstances in which the use of each would be most appropriate (Cambridge Scholarship).
3. For which reasons may it be in a country's interest to impose a tariff on imported goods? (Cambridge Scholarship).
4. 'If a country is fully employed, but has a deficit on the current account of the balance of payments, the deficit can be wiped out only by reducing consumption and investment at home.' Explain and Discuss (O. & C. 'A').
5. What are the sterling balances? How do changes in the sterling balances affect the U.K. balance of payments? (O. & C. 'A').
6. Britain's share in world trade has been falling in recent years. Discuss the causes and consequences of this change (O. & C. 'A').
7. What was the importance of shipping to the British economy between 1875 and 1914? (O. & C. Economic History 'A').
8. Why is the balance of payments so persistently a problem to British Governments? (O. & C. 'A').

9. 'If we join the Common Market, there will be more trade and therefore more crises in the balance of payments.' Discuss.
10. Was the First World War the major reason for Britain's depressed trade in the inter-war years? (London Econ. Hist. 'A').
11. 'Britain could, with advantage, have adopted protection in the early twentieth century, by 1931 she had no choice.' Discuss (London Econ. Hist. 'A').
12. The Government has been attempting to stimulate home production of goods that would otherwise be imported. Do you believe that such 'import substitution' would lead to the best allocation of resources? (O. & C. Special).
13. Would you expect the devaluation of a national currency to contribute substantially towards reducing a balance of payments deficit? (O. & C. Special).
14. The net balance on British invisible trade has been declining in recent years. Why is this and what is its significance to the British balance of payments? (J.M.B. 'A').
15. A country with a balance of payments deficit is sometimes described as a 'country that is spending more than it is earning.' Does that seem to you to be a satisfactory description? (Oxford School).
16. What are the causes of the fluctuations in a country's balance of payments from one year to the next? (J.M.B.).
17. What were the chief causes and consequences of Britain's abandonment of the Gold Standard in 1931? (W.J.E.C. 'A' level).
18. Account for the rapid growth of British exports in the third quarter of the nineteenth century (London Econ. Hist. 'A').
19. Why was the difference between the rates of growth of world industrial production and of international trade so much wider between 1919 and 1939 than between 1880 and 1914? (B.Sc. (Econ.) Part 1).
20. Why does Britain's growth performance in exports compare unfavourably with those of most of the leading industrial nations in the last 20 years?

INDEX